MORE ESSAYS ON BOOKS

MORE ESSAYS ON BOOKS

BY

A. CLUTTON-BROCK

Essay Index Reprint Series

BOOKS FOR LIBRARIES PRESS
FREEPORT, NEW YORK

First Published 1921
Reprinted 1968

LIBRARY OF CONGRESS CATALOG CARD NUMBER:

68-57313

PRINTED IN THE UNITED STATES OF AMERICA

PREFACE

THESE Essays, like those in the first series, are reprinted from the *Times Literary Supplement*. One or two reviewers accused the essays in the first series of optimism, by which they seem to have meant the absence of pessimism. I hope they will find the same fault with the second.

A. CLUTTON-BROCK

GODALMING
April 2, 1921

PREFACE

CONTENTS

MORE ESSAYS ON BOOKS

Walt Whitman ∽ ∽ ∽ ∽ ∽

WE are past surprise at Walt Whitman now, past the first tittering and partisanship. We are used to his art, his character, his doctrine ; yet we have not made up our minds about him, and for the time his case stands over. About his very method we are doubtful ; he succeeds with it often enough ; but we are not sure whether he made the best of himself with it, whether he was not wilful in his refusal to attempt a more difficult way. And, as it is with his method, so it is with his doctrine. As he tries to shout himself into poetry, so he tries to shout himself into faith and joy ; but is there behind all this shouting a fear lest he should break down if he were to stop and think ?

Reading him again, one doubts whether he has told the whole truth even about himself as

A   I

known to himself. He must have had more
misgivings ; not merely misgivings of cowardice,
but those searchings of the heart that make
for subtlety, tenderness, and faith. A man can
cut himself off in life, as in art, from infinity ;
he can aim at a lower success ; and did
Whitman aim at a lower success in both ? He
resolves what he will believe, as how he will
write, and then with an obstinate "will to
power" carries out his resolve. He says to
himself and to all men, "Thy sins be forgiven
thee." But the question asks itself—Are they
forgiven after all ? "Clear and sweet is my
soul, and clear and sweet is all that is not my
soul." Say that often and loudly enough, and
will it be true ? If you make it true for yourself, have you not lost something ? Not in
Whitman's language nor in his mood would it
be possible to write *King Lear* or *Hamlet*, or
any equivalent to them ; what is more, he has
cut himself, and any follower of his, off from
the possibility of writing anything in that vein
or with that beauty, however inferior. He is
different in kind from writers of the first order,
as Rubens from Michelangelo, different not
only in power, but in possibility. There are
much smaller writers who yet have written a
single lyric far beyond his best, because they

Walt Whitman

had always the highest in mind. He had not; his way of writing, as of thinking and feeling, is a makeshift, a despair of perfection. He is at the opposite extreme to an epigrammatist in the Greek Anthology; but there is something to be said for Meleager and against him.

But since Whitman has done many things well, why complain that he has not done them better? The answer is that one cannot separate his art from his doctrine, for it is a part of his doctrine. He willed to write as he willed to think and feel; his method was a part of his conduct, its very manners were the manners of a democrat in literature according to his conception of democracy. So we are right to ask whether or no this method, like this doctrine, is capable of producing the highest; for, if not, mankind will never be content with it. It is no excuse to say of an artist that he is a pioneer; we know now that Giotto is to be valued, not because he was a pioneer, but because he was Giotto. His art would have been forgotten if it had not a positive and absolute excellence; and it has that because he was aiming at the highest possible in art and did sometimes achieve it. So it is with doctrine; it also must aim at the highest possible, like the Sermon on the Mount;

3

but can we accept Whitman's doctrine as aiming at the highest possible? Is it not at its best a mere release, a reaction, a getting rid of litter and lumber; and is not that also true of his way of writing? Compare him, for instance, with Poe. Poe has no inspiriting doctrine; in his art he does not "free himself from feudal fetters"; but is there in all the *Leaves of Grass* anything that moves us like *The Sleeper?* Tolstoy, no doubt, would say that we ought to like *Leaves of Grass* best; but in the matter of art there are no oughts. The wind bloweth where it listeth. There was in Poe the passion for perfection, not for release or reform; he was half pedant, but the other half divine poet. Whitman's voice, compared with his, is hoarse and strained, as if he were speaking to a crowd, not whispering to himself what he had heard from some enchanted distance. The Grace of God sometimes descends on Poe, but if ever it descends on Whitman, he must himself comment on it and point its moral.

Besides, Whitman sets out to be a philosopher, however much he might himself dislike the word. The first of his Inscriptions begins:—

One's Self I sing, a simple separate person,
Yet utter the word Democratic, the word
En-Masse.

4

Walt Whitman

He is always, and consciously, concerned with the problem of the Universal and the Particular; and he is a mystic in his solution of it. That is to say, he insists on his own experience that they are one, if only you see them both intensely enough. It is not by arguing that you can reach the truth, but by attaining to it in Heaven-sent moments. The mystic always appeals to experience, Whitman says. You may talk as you choose, but I know. So the statement of the mystic should be art rather than philosophy: his business is to draw the truth he has seen so that we may see it and be convinced by it. But often Whitman does not draw it, he merely talks about it, as in the lines we have quoted; he tells us that it is so again and again, as if we would accept his authority for it, when what we need is his art.

So he has got a great part of his popularity from those who were grateful to him for saying so firmly and so often what they wished to believe. He did free them from old bogies; and, if it were possible for mankind permanently to believe anything because it makes them feel cheerful, he would be permanently a great philosopher, a great divine. But the history of thought and of religion proves that men cannot permanently believe anything because it makes them feel cheerful; indeed, they have a strange turn for believing, with little or no reason, what makes them feel miserable. They are irrationally haunted by bogies and primeval fears, from which Whitman would free them by shouting loud and cheerfully. There he is like Browning; and sometimes both irritate us, as if they were cheerful old men saying that it is a bright fresh morning when we ourselves shiver in the bitter east wind; their philosophy seems only the result of a good circulation. But we want a philosophy and a religion true for all men and for ever :—

I say no man has ever yet been half devout
    enough,
None has ever yet adored or worshipped half
    enough,
None has begun to think how divine he himself is,
    and how certain the future is.

We can believe that doctrine when it is expressed in music, when it carries its certainty in its own beauty; but Whitman's mere " I say " is not enough, except for those who have the will to believe already.

So much against Whitman, which needs to be said now if we are to reach his real truth and beauty ; for we can reach them only when we have seen through his willed cheerfulness. He was a man not strong enough in art or in life to do without that willed cheerfulness ; it is for him a defence like irony, though a newer, more democratic, more American defence. Because the Americans are a nervous people, easily cast down, they will to be always bright and cheerful and practise smiling outwardly so that they may smile inwardly. They have a method of living always up to their own story ; and Whitman does in *Leaves of Grass* live always up to his own story of the universe with a wonderful American innocence ; but read them carefully, and you will often find in them the pathos of a bright American mother still smiling though her child is dead. In spite of himself and his doctrine that all is well for ever and ever, still he cannot refrain from pity and tears :—

O Captain, my Captain, rise up and hear the
    bells ;
Rise up—for you the flag is flung—for you the
    bugle trills,
For you bouquets and ribbon'd wreaths—for you
    the shores a-crowding,
For you they call, the swaying mass, their eager
    faces turning ;

More Essays on Books

Here Captain, dear father!
This arm beneath your head!
   It is some dream that on the deck
   You've fallen cold and dead.

Clumsily he returns to the old forms to express the old grief he cannot and would not expel with his new philosophy. Still men die and still we must mourn for them, not in cheerful catalogues, but in music; and Whitman takes up the old fiddle and plays on it like a beginner because, as it was the fiddle his fathers played, so he feels the unanswerable sorrow they felt.

More than philosophy, art tells us the truth; for the most sincere philosopher tells it consciously, but the artist tells it unconsciously. He need make no apology for the universe; he need not trick even himself into believing that he is happier than he is. And so Whitman tells the truth most about himself, and about life, when he is most an artist. His best poems are those nearest in rhythm to ordinary verse:—

   The moon gives you light,
And the bugles and the drums give you music,
And my heart, O my soldiers, my veterans,
   My heart gives you love.

He is most serious when most musical, when surprised by events out of his will to be cheer-

8

ful, when the universal rhythm beats through
his words. *The Song of Myself* is a very
interesting essay; you can agree with it here,
and there disagree; sometimes you feel that
Whitman is very laboriously making a fool of
himself in it, like a man who wears absurd
clothes on principle; sometimes you are surprised by a satire like that of Christ upon the
Pharisees, as in the famous lines in praise of
animals :—

They do not sweat and whine about their condi-
tion.
They do not lie awake in the dark and weep for
their sins,
They do not make me sick discussing their duty to
God,
Not one is dissatisfied, not one is demented with
the mania of owning things,
Not one kneels to another, nor to his kind that
lived thousands of years ago.
Not one is respectable or unhappy over the whole
earth.

But then we remember that some of the
greatest men, such as St. Augustine, have
lain awake in the dark and wept for their sins,
and also that we do not know enough about
animals to say what Whitman says about
them. In them, too, there may be the begin-
nings of penitence, of property, of snobbery

even; it is only that they cannot talk to us about these things. But these doubts do not arise over the *Dirge for Two Veterans* or over *Pioneers*; in them the rhythm carries our whole mind with it. They tell us of Whitman's real values, not of his creed. It was the war and Lincoln that moved him beyond his principles; they tore his heart, they made him live and feel, not according to rule, but to a music not his own—

Spirit whose work is done—spirit of dreadful hours,
Ere departing fade from my eyes your forests of bayonets.
Spirit of gloomiest fears and doubts (Yet onward ever unfaltering pressing),
Spirit of many a solemn day and many a savage scene—electric spirit,
That with muttering voice through the war now closed, like a tireless phantom flitting,————
Touch my mouth ere you depart.

That spirit did touch his mouth. We hear it if we read him now, when we too have known the same dreadful hours and won a victory in which we cannot exult. To Liberty he says :—

Lo in these hours supreme,
No poem proud I chanting bring thee, nor mastery's rapturous verse,

Walt Whitman

But a cluster containing night's darkness and
   blood-dripping wounds,
And psalms of the dead.

There his method justifies itself and expresses
his own mind. The war, as he saw it and felt
it so close, was beyond art for him, beyond
beauty, beyond a song of victory. He thought
and spoke of the cost of it, and had just faith
enough to believe that the cost was not too
great. But no pacifist could reproach him
with an easy acceptance of war, though
in other poems one might reproach him
with a too easy acceptance of life. The weak
point of his philosophy is that in proclaiming
all things good he is in danger of emptying all
things of value. But, when he speaks of war,
this danger is gone. Then he knows that
there is evil indeed which cannot be outfaced
by high spirits. And we know as we read him
that he did outface it with something better,
with sorrow and pity and forgiveness. Perhaps
he never spoke so seriously or with a beauty so
hard-won as in the poem called Reconcilia-
tion :—

Word over all, beautiful as the sky,
Beautiful that war and all its deeds of carnage
   must in time be utterly lost,

That the hand of the sisters Death and Night
  incessantly softly wash again, and ever again,
  this soiled world ;
For my enemy is dead, a man divine as myself is
  dead,
I look where he lies white-faced and still in the
  coffin—I draw near,
Bend down and touch lightly with my lips the
  white face in the coffin.

We might learn from that how to think, and
feel, of a conquered enemy, so that we, too,
may reach a peace of the mind. There is in
Whitman's war poems not a base or silly or
dishonest word. He does not pretend that
soldiers are always grinning, or that they drive
the enemy before them like sheep. He knew
the hospitals and the pain in them, of Federals
and Confederates alike :—

Bearing the bandages, water and sponge,
Straight and swift to my wounded I go,
Where they lie on the ground after the battle
  brought in.

That is what he says he remembers of the war.
" Was one side so brave ? the other was
equally brave." In the hospital there is no
enemy but death—

Young man, I think I know you—I think this face
  is the face of the Christ himself,
Dead and divine and brother of all, and here
  again he lies.

Walt Whitman

As we read those lines, we think of another curious, absurd, line of his—

The Union always swarming with blatherers and always sure and impregnable.

And at last we understand his peculiar tolerance even of himself. He might have answered to what we have said against him that his *Leaves of Grass* swarmed with blather, that he himself was half a fool, and yet, because he knew it, impregnable and safe.

13

George Herbert   ✑   ✑   ✑   ✑

IN the preface to his edition of Herbert, Mr. Palmer says that there are few to whom it will seem worth while, " but its aim is lavishness"; he was named after Herbert by a lover of Herbert, and knew a large part of his verse before he could read. " I could not die in peace if I did not raise a costly monument to his beneficent memory."

He himself, he tells us, is a Puritan and often repelled by Herbert's elaborate ecclesiasticism; but the New England Puritan of to-day keeps the cleanness and sweetness of seventeenth-century piety, transplanted across the Atlantic and there naturalized and still thriving. That piety was clean and sweet because it was intellectual, never content to hypnotize itself with old formulas, or to imitate sexual infatuation with religious ecstasy. Reason kept it modest; and this modesty the New England Puritan admires and shares. It is not mere innocence and

14

prettiness, because it is always restlessly intellectual, richer not poorer in content than
mere rapture, more full of experience, more
interesting and, when it attains to beauty,
more beautiful. Mr. Palmer says that Herbert
even now, when his name is respected, is more
bought than read. "Half a dozen of his
poems are famous; but the remainder, many
of them equally fitted for household words,
nobody looks at." We do not know whether
this is true, but we do know that he is one of
the most interesting of poets, one who can be
read in a prosaic mood, and the reading of
whom will lift one gently out of that mood to
the height of his own sudden yet not incon-
gruous beauties.

Mr. Palmer prints in his text no readings
from the Williams MS. discovered by Dr.
Grosart. He believes, rightly, we think, that
this MS. represents an earlier text which
Herbert afterwards altered in many details;
and he is also right, no doubt, to accept
Herbert's own changes. But we do not agree
with him that they were always for the better.
The text of the Williams MS. is rougher, but
often more vigorous. Herbert seems sometimes to have been afraid of his own vigour,
and to have smoothed it away. Thus in *The*

Church Porch the second stanza in the text is—

Beware of lust : it doth pollute and foul
  Whom God in Baptisme washt with his own
    blood.
It blots thy lesson written in thy soul ;
The holy lines cannot be understood.
How dare those eyes upon a Bible look,
Much lesse towards God, whose lust is all their
    book ?

But in the Williams MS. it runs—

Beware of lust (startle not), O beware,
It makes thy soule a blott ; it is a rodd
Whose twigs are pleasures, and they whip thee
    bare.
It spoils an Angel : robs thee of thy God.

It seems to me that the later version is more "parsonic," more merely edifying than the first, which says more and with more force and precision. In fact, if there were question which reading was genuine, I should choose the earlier. But Mr. Palmer gives all the readings of the Williams MS., so that we can take our choice.

The common notion of Herbert is false, and must be based on small knowledge of his life and poetry ; it is, indeed, calculated to rob his poetry of interest.

George Herbert

"Often he is pictured as an aged saint who, through spending a lifetime in priestly offices, has come to find interest only in devout emotions. . . . In reality Herbert died under forty; was a priest less than three years, spent his remaining thirty-six years among men who loved power, place, wit, pleasure, and learning; and held his own among them remarkably well."

Herbert himself said when dying that his poems were "a picture of the many spiritual conflicts that have passed betwixt God and my soul, before I could submit mine to the will of Jesus my Master"; and this was not "the last deliberate snuffle of a blameless prig," but a true account of them. He is an interesting poet because this conflict in his life was real and because he expressed it in his verse. It was a conflict between ambition and beauty; he saw more and more clearly that worldliness is ugly, yet he could not rid his mind of it. There were in him the courtier and the artist, and only gradually and painfully did the artist win. Nowadays the artist would not express himself like Herbert; but he would feel the same temptations and need the same renunciation, not for nothingness, but for the beauty that is his deepest and most permanent desire. Some artists never have to make the choice; beauty is to them the only temptation; the world does not exist except as an outside enemy. But for Herbert it was an enemy within, and that is why he fortifies himself with incessant self-analysis, why he must be telling himself, sometimes dully and with too much argument, that beauty, which he calls God, is his true desire.

Like his master Donne, he is not an easy, confident lover of beauty; he will not throw himself into the poet's attitude and trust to rhythms or poetic words to inspire him; he begins with prose and labours upwards to poetry. No poet is more conscious of the double problem of art, the counterpoint of sense and music. There is Donne between him and the Elizabethan lyric, with its predominance of music so great that it makes the problem of art almost single; and his contempt of love-poetry is as much æsthetic as moral. Love seems to him too easy an incitement to verse:—

> Roses and lilies speak Thee: and to make
> A pair of cheeks of them, is Thy abuse.
> Why should I women's eyes for Chrystal take?
> Such poor invention burns in their low mind
> Whose fire is wild and doth not upward go
> To praise, and on Thee, Lord, some ink bestow.
> Open the bones, and you shall nothing find
> In the best face but filth; when, Lord, in Thee
> The beauty lies in the discovery.

George Herbert

That last line expresses his whole poetic faith and method; for him beauty always lies, and is achieved, in discovery; it is to be sought where you would not expect to find it, and wrought of unwilling materials.

Thousands of notions in my brain did runne,
Offering their service if I were not sped.
I often blotted what I had begunne ;
This was not quick enough and that was dead.
Nothing could seem too rich to clothe the sunne,
Much less those joyes which trample on his head.

As flames do work and wind when they ascend,
So did I weave myself into the sense.
But while I bustled, I might heare a friend
Whisper—How wide is all this long pretence !
There is in love a sweetness readie penn'd ;
Copie out only that and save expense.

Here he describes his own method and also criticizes it ; he longs for a sweetness ready penned, but will not pretend to it when he has not achieved it. Beauty ought to take the pen and write for him ; but he must train himself to be her servant and must not find her where she is not. So behind his piety, or pietism, there is always the artist's problem and the artist's labours, though he does not believe in art for art's sake. He would do all things for the glory of God ; but he sees that it is not only duty but also beauty, and beauty made more exact and profound by duty.

Herbert is not one of those poets who lose themselves in the richness of the external world or can satisfy themselves in expressing it. The external throws him back into himself, and then his thoughts turn outwards for confirmation. Beauty troubles him with his own inadequacy, and to escape from that he seeks again for beauty. He is, in the language of modern psychology, both introvert and extrovert, yet never an egotist. For his problem is always universal, the problem not of himself and his own salvation but of all mankind; and in the poems that express his most intense experience we recognize our own, heightened and elucidated, though the terms of his expression may not be what we should choose.

How should I praise thee, Lord. How should my
    rymes
  Gladly engrave thy love in steel,
If what my soul does feel sometimes,
  My soul might ever feel!

Although there were some fourtie heavens, or more,
  Sometimes I peer above them all;
Sometimes I hardly reach a score,
  Sometimes to hell I fall.

George Herbert

That expresses all the insecurity, not merely
of human joy, but of human incapacity. "We
live in a world where too much is required,"
and Herbert consents to this tax upon the
spirit, and justifies it in words that are con-
vincing in their beauty :—

> Yet take thy way, for sure thy way is best,
> Stretch or contract me thy poore debter.
> This is but tuning of my breast,
> To make the music better.

Still more intimate and closer to actual experience is *The Flower*, with that famous verse
which seems written for every man who tries
to live the life of the spirit :—

> And now in age I bud again,
> After so many deaths I live and write ;
> I once more smell the dew and rain,
> And relish versing. O my onely light,
>   It cannot be
>   That I am he
> On whom thy tempests fell all night.

Herbert's poems are the autobiography of a
mind with a rich and difficult content. He
himself says as much ; though he may call himself a sinner, he has not the 'umbleness of Uriah
Heep, but seems to take a pride in the diversity
of his unregenerate experience. He is a sinner
worth saving—one who knows the worth of
what he renounces :—

I know the ways of pleasure, the sweet strains,
  The lullings and the relishes of it ;
The propositions of hot blood and brains ;
  What mirth and music mean ; what love and wit
Have done these twentie hundred years and
    more ;
  I know the projects of unbridled store ;
My stuffe is flesh, not brasse ; my senses live,
And grumble oft that they have more in me
    Than he that curbs them, being but one to
    five ;
          Yet I love Thee.

Here he shows himself one of the cleverest of
poets, as clever as Browning ; with all the arts
of prose, yet with the momentum and con-
trolling power of poetry. It is a misfortune
that he should be known mainly by a few
simple lyrics and outrageous quaintnesses, as if
he were half a child and half a pedant. The
phrase "Quaint old Herbert" misdescribes
him completely. He was always young, and
his thought is less old-fashioned than that of
most poets of the eighteenth or even the nineteenth century. What seems old-fashioned to
us is the disregard of poetic usage, the homeli-
ness which he never tries to avoid, because
poetry for him is in the subject-matter and
the effort to express it, not in select words or
images. He will say what he has to say by

George Herbert

whatever means he can find, and he seldom fails to say it. He may surprise us, but, unless we are conventionally fastidious, we enjoy the surprise; for often beyond it there is beauty, the more delightful for the unexpected means by which it is achieved. Few poets are so continually interesting, for in few do we so often recognize truth. If Herbert were a painter, we should say that he could draw; there is nothing in his verse evaded or left vague; he gives us a good likeness of experience, and is a master of circumstance, never mastered by it. Details are there full and exact, but controlled by the purpose and theme; indeed, few poets have such cumulative power or such a command of real form. The prose virtues are his but in subordination; he will not lose them in music, but his music persists through them, often difficult to grasp, sometimes harsh and laboured, but always serious, and at any moment likely to surge up in divine sweetness. It is never safe to reject a poem of Herbert's as a failure; the failure may be in you, and with another attempt you may discover a secret beauty which seems all the more beautiful for having lain hid so long. This Mr. Palmer knows by long intimacy with his favourite poet, and his edition should help others to the same intimacy.

George Meredith ✎ ✎ ✎ ✎

I. THE NOVELS

THE English novel has never had any steady or consistent development. Each of our greater novelists stands only for himself; and none of them is so completely isolated as Meredith. He neither began nor ended any movement in the English novel. You cannot call him either a romantic or a realist, except by using one of those terms in an unusual sense. He is not a romantic, in that he never revolts or flinches from reality. He delights in things as they are, and his one aim is to express the essence of them. But he is not a realist, in that he never labours to convey any illusion of reality, never tries to tell a story as if he had experienced it all himself. He does not, like Tolstoy, find all facts significant and all people interesting. He is fastidious about both; and the aim of his whole process is to eliminate the ordinary, or, if he treats it at all,

24

to treat it only as it appears to an extra-ordinary mind.

In this he is like Shakespeare, who has the same passion for extraordinary characters and for intense experience, and who, in the same way, introduces the ordinary, whether in char-acters or in events, as a foil to the extra-ordinary. Meredith is in his novels nearer to poetry than any other of our novelists; and that is the reason why he is constantly in difficulties with his form. For his tendency is not towards narrative poetry, but towards lyrical, and lyrical poetry interrupts the flow even of an epic or of a drama, and is incon-gruous with the process of a prose narrative. Scott also was a poet; but when he comes near to poetry in his novels it is narrative poetry, and only heightens instead of interrupt-ing his story. But Meredith is one of those great men to be found in every art who are not content with its limitations. When he wrote poetry he was not content with the ex-pression of emotion as his main purpose. He must reason as well, must make poetry do the work of prose without ever becoming prosaic. And in his stories he was not content only to tell a story or even to make the telling of it his chief aim. He wished also to express the emotion provoked by every situation with the personal intensity of a lyrical poet. Often when he does this, as in the famous " Diversion played on a penny whistle" in *Richard Feverel*, the characters seem to fade away, and there remains only the poet speaking to us in a music freed from all circumstance of time and place.

It is the same with his wit, as irrepressible as his poetry. The poetry comes when he wishes to make an emotional comment on his story ; the wit when his comment is intellectual. And it is often just as abstract, just as free from all circumstance, as the poetry, even when he puts it into the mouth of one of his characters. In nearly all his novels there is some character whom we recognize as soon as he appears as the author's mouthpiece for intellectual comment. Mr. Bernard Shaw has the same trick, but his mouthpieces are often his heroes. They are godlike, knowing the secret of life and explaining it to the anger and bewilderment of the other characters. Meredith's mouthpieces are always subsidiary and often unpleasant; like the wise youth in *Richard Feverel*. One feels that if one of his heroes had a turn for epigrams he could never be got to do anything except emit them.

26

George Meredith

So he would never make a hero more witty than he could help, for he likes his heroes to be either men of action or delightful youths whom too much cleverness would spoil. He himself was not in love with cleverness and never aimed at it; he could not help it; it was a trick with him, like stammering; it was even an impediment to his speech.

No one can read any of his novels, except perhaps *Evan Harrington*, without feeling that the writer is all the while fighting his way through impediments. He never, like some of his imitators, raises them so that he may set himself the task of climbing over them. He does not think much of these witty characters that he cannot do without. They have to be there because wit is his natural comment upon life, like poetry, and because he is as much a commentator as a creator. He chose the novel as his chief form of art not because he was a born story-teller, though he can tell stories well enough when he chooses, but because he needed a form loose enough to give employment to all the varied and conflicting activities of his mind. If he had had less genius, less power of speech, less understanding of men, he might have been an essayist; we cannot imagine a smaller Meredith a novelist at all.

Without that prodigious energy all the various
elements of his novels would fly apart; a
lesser man could not have kept them together,
and would have lost his story altogether in
comment and rhapsody. As it is the story
often stops, not from lack of driving power,
but like a mill that has too much material
poured into it. Meredith's very conception
never takes the form of continuous narrative.
We may conjecture that he saw a novel as a
series of situations, much as Wagner saw an
opera, and that his main difficulty was to jump
from one to another with as little matter-of-
fact explanation as possible. He is impatient
of the machinery necessary to bring his situations about, so impatient that he often hides it
among coruscations of wit, and the reader has
to turn back to see how a situation suddenly
sprung on him has been contrived. And when
he reaches a situation he exults in it and dwells
upon it, conjuring up all the glories of heaven
and earth to second the delight of his lovers,
until the lovers themselves are lost in the
splendour of that transfigured state of being.
Beauchamp's Career and *Richard Feverel* are,
in their love passages, as near to opera as it
is possible for any prose narrative to be, and
Harry Richmond ought to have made a

libretto for Mozart. That, perhaps, is the
novel which he wrote with most gusto; there
is more invention in it than in any other, and
it is just far enough away from reality to provide easy opportunities for the exercise of all
his gifts. It is almost as far from reality as a
Shakespeare comedy; and Richmond Roy reminds us of Shakespeare's characters in general,
though not of any one of them in particular.
And it is worth noting that this masterpiece
consists altogether of variations upon one
situation. The relation between the father
and son begins in the very first chapter, and
nearly every incident is another example of it.
There is but little development; from first to
last the hero, as ordinary a man as any to be
found among Meredith's characters, struggles
impotently among the complications produced
by his extraordinary father, and they only end
with his father's characteristic and symbolic
death.

No one but Meredith or Shakespeare could
have produced a masterpiece with such a theme,
for no one else would have had the necessary
invention. Richmond Roy is to him a pretext
for the exercise of all his phantasy, as Don
Giovanni is a pretext to Mozart for the musical
expression of every emotion. He is the centre

of a number of different situations which are linked together by the fact that he is the only begetter of them; and on him Meredith squanders all his powers of expression. He is described from a dozen points of view; and Squire Beltham's description, which is the most hostile, reminds one of the encounters between Falstaff and Prince Hal, for Beltham curses Roy with his own prodigality. No one ever did talk like that; indeed, nothing in the book has any resemblance to the routine of life; but it is a state of being heightened, like the state of being represented in a great opera, by the delight of its creator in describing it. We do not expect to find this kind of delight in a·novel, or the virtuosity which is the invariable expression of it. We are used nowadays to novelists who write like sad and patient men, who seem to be doing their best to bear up against the world they describe. Novels are written in prose, and many writers think that the chief virtue of prose is to be prosaic. Meredith, we may believe, only wrote prose novels because that happened to be the narrative form of his age. We can imagine how, if he had lived in the time of Elizabeth, he would have exulted in the poetic drama. No doubt his plays would have been loose in construction, but they could not have been looser than some of Shakespeare's, and he would have made a new thing of the Elizabethan fool. That drama would have suited him as well as any conceivable form could; he was not so well suited by the novel, for there was nothing in it to restrain his richness of comment or to control and direct his invention. We may believe that if Shakespeare lived now and wrote novels—he could hardly write anything else—he would play just as many tricks with his narrative as Meredith played. Though he was a practical playwright, whose business was to make plays that would act, he could not avoid the obscurity that comes of rich and complicated processes of thought. Meredith, for the greater part of his life, was not a practical novelist—that is to say, his novels did not sell—and we cannot believe that he ever wrote with the aim of selling them. In this, no doubt, he was right; but if, like Shakespeare, he had written for an audience to whom poetry was one of the ordinary pleasures of life, it would have been a wholesome discipline for him. He had no such audience, and therefore he wrote to please himself, and to say whatever his story might suggest to his wonderful mind. Certainly he could tell a story.

The duel in *Vittoria* is as fine a piece of narrative as ever was written. Whenever he liked he could create living men and women, and he could set them acting as well as any novelist. But their action roused him at once to such intellectual activity that he would often cease to be a novelist in the midst of it and become a poet or a wit.

Thus all his defects come from excess of power, excess of invention, emotion, and specu-lation. And he is sometimes obscure because he tries to be story-teller and poet and wit all at once. The very structure of his sentences is often the result of this attempt, and he dazzles and bewilders like a juggler playing with three balls. It has been said that there is pedantry and affectation in his wit. Affectation is an easy explanation of anything extraordinary and a word as vague as it is offensive. Yet we may admit that his wit, like Shakespeare's, is not always happy. Some-times he seems to have a fit of being witty and cannot leave off. He will take a theme, like the remark about Sir Willoughby Patterne's leg, and work it out as if he were composing a fugue on it, persisting even when all his invention is exhausted. But as all wit arises in the attempt to surmount some kind of

George Meredith

difficulty, to say a rude thing politely, or an improper thing properly, so his wit arises usually in the attempt to say three different things at once; and he is forced to attempt this because, if he said all that he wanted to say at length, his novels would never come to an end. He is never difficult because his ideas are confused or vague or uncertain. He knew what he valued in life, and what life meant to him. At bottom his characters and his situations are simple. His complexity is only of process, of the attempt to tell a story, to express the emotions aroused by it, and to comment upon them, all at the same time. Like all great writers he is capable of simplicity when he chooses; and his simplicity tells the more, like Shakespeare's, because it is rare, and because, when it comes, it is the result, not of pure emotion like a song of Schubert's, but of emotion for the moment mastering all the restless play of his intellect and forcing it into concord, as a tune entering in a symphony will seem suddenly to master all the instruments that have just before been quarrelling, and to sweep them all together into its own impetus.

It must be confessed that his novels seldom produce the illusion of reality, and then

not for long. But must we assume that the
first business of a novel, any more than of a
picture, is to convey the illusion of reality ?
Pictures vary infinitely in the extent of their
illusion; and so no doubt may any kind of
representative art, even prose narrative. If
his novels are not like life itself, no more are
the pictures of Tintoret. Life is too much
heightened and explained in them to be like
reality ; we can always see the hand of the
master and feel the power and strain of his
process of creation. He shows us a god's
factory of life rather than life itself, in which
the god is for ever making new experiments
and expressing with divine energy his own
delight in them. Meredith never, like Tolstoy,
tells a story as if he, the teller of it, were a
mere man. He seems to know what it all
means better than any man could ; and to all
his characters he seems to impart his own
energy and splendour of expression. Thus he
acts upon us directly like music, which cannot
convey any illusion, rather than indirectly
through the illusion of reality, as all kinds of
drama and narrative are supposed to do. But
he does act upon us as only great artists
can.

34

George Meredith ✎ ✎ ✎ ✎

II.—THE POETRY

SINCE Meredith was a poet, his technical peculiarities are the expression of certain peculiarities of his mind. He was always an experimenter in poetry, and his experiments in form are but symptoms of experiments in matter. His poetry has often a strange sound, because he tried to introduce new processes into the making of poetry; because, like Donne, he attempted to combine emotion, which is the proper subject-matter of poetry, with an exercise of the reason, which is the proper subject-matter of prose. Like Donne, he was not a prosaic poet; he never treated verse as a more ornamental and difficult form of prose. But emotion in his poetry, like action in his novels, instantly provoked him to speculation; and the effort to express emotion and simultaneously to reason about it often produced verse difficult in sense and broken in music.

35

More Essays on Books

The development of poetry, as of all art, is seldom regular. It proceeds by reactions and experiments, often half-fruitless. The qualities of any great movement in poetry quickly betray their defects, and a new generation takes a disgust of both. Poetry, naturally and normally, is closely connected both with music and speech; and Elizabethan poetry, being very normal, was half-song and half-rhetoric. Donne took a disgust both of its tunes and of its rhetoric. His aim was to write verse in which sense would not be carried away by sound or diluted into fine phrases. He was suspicious of familiar rhythms; for it seemed to him that what the individual had to say could not be fitted to a popular tune. It was his determination not to tamper with his own sense, and not any lack of inspiration, that made his music so uncertain. Meredith reacted from the romantic poets much as Donne reacted from the Elizabethans; he was suspicious of romantic tunes and romantic rhetoric. That cry of his for more brain applied to poetry as well as to conduct; he was determined that his brain should not be lulled to sleep by his own music; rather it should question every beauty of words like an *advocatus diaboli* that will let none pass unless it can

George Meredith

prove its relevance to an intellectual process. Already in *Modern Love* the conflict between reason and emotion has begun. The poet, as if to silence all questioning of his capacity, proves himself again and again a master of the old music. He can start a sonnet like Shakespeare himself :—

Out in the yellow meadows, where the bee
Hums by us with the honey of the Spring,
And showers of sweet notes from the larks on
 wing
Are dropping like a noon-dew, wander we.
Or is it now? or was it then? for now,
As then, the larks from running rings pour showers :
The golden foot of May is on the flowers,
And friendly shadows dance upon her brow.

But questions are creeping in already ; and for him, as for his mouthpiece, this is the music of the past, which he makes half-ironically to point the contrast with the troubled present.

Now, as then, the grace
Of heaven seems holding earth in its embrace.

But he is not content to take all these shows of beauty at their surface value, and to sing of them like a bird ; nor can he use all the powers of his mind to heighten delight or to keep up the pretence that he feels the whole universe to be one harmony of music.

37

A kiss is but a kiss now! and no wave
Of a great flood that whirls me to the sea.
But, as you will! we'll sit contentedly,
And eat our pot of honey on the grave.

That is what the decadent poets of the Greek
Anthology and of all time do. They pretend
to an outworn faith so that they may still
make beauty out of it. But, needless to say,
Meredith was not one of them. He would
not surrender the freedom of his mind to his
art. For the moment he could say: "God,
what a dancing spectre seems the moon"; but
he would not allow his poetry to be also a
dancing spectre. The struggle between beauty
and the rebellious intellect must be fought
out, however doubtful the issue.

That struggle was maintained through all
his poetry; and whenever beauty prevails in
it she is still breathless. But what strength
and determination the struggle gives her! She
is never an odalisque to weary us with luxurious
sweetness and studied charms; she has always
to fight for her life, and often reveals herself
most clearly while fighting. For Meredith,
though he might chasten beauty, loved her
passionately, as we know by a hundred proofs.
In *Love in the Valley* he surrendered himself
to her, almost as Spenser did in his *Epithal-*

amion; and then he made a music as new
and irresistible as the music of *Atalanta*.
Love in the Valley is a romantic poem indeed,
the subject being the very essence of romance,
first love, shy, wondering, and yet undoubt-
ing, that transfigures heaven and earth like a
May morning or a summer night. It is a
theme that inspired the music of the first
folk-songs, and there is all the accumulated
richness of the past in Meredith's treatment
of it. The verse itself has for its underlying
tune the old Saturnian measure—

"The Queen was in her parlour eating bread and
    honey."
"Under yonder beech-tree single on the green-
    sward."

It is a measure that haunts the ears of modern
poets like the old tune of bells, so that they
all play with it—Tennyson in "All along the
Valley, stream that flashest white"; Browning
in a pretty song in *Ferishtah's Fancies*:—

Round us the wild creatures, overhead the trees,
Underfoot the moss-tracks—life and love with these!

Yet with all of them it is a tune for variations,
for they cannot keep to its simplicity; and in
Love in the Valley new and wonderful tunes
come of the variations. But there is singing
music all through, with an accompaniment of

all the sounds of summer. It is folk-song with
the modern orchestra like the symphonies of
Dvorák, and it combines a singing rhythm
with sharpness and fulness of detail as they
had never before been combined in romantic
poetry.

Yellow with birdfoot-trefoil are the grass-glades;
   Yellow with cinque-foil of the dew-grey leaf;
Yellow with stonecrop; the moss-mounds are yellow;
   Blue-necked the wheat sways, yellowing to the
      sheaf.
Green-yellow bursts from the copse the laughing
      yaffle;
   Sharp as a sickle is the edge of shade and shine:
Earth in her heart laughs looking at the heavens,
   Thinking of the harvest: I look and think of
      mine.

In *Phœbus with Admetus* the Saturnian metre
is again the basis, and it has a folk-song theme
treated with all the fuller consciousness, but
without any of the unreality, of modern art.
And again all the sharp and crowded details
are mastered by the music :—

Chirping none the scarlet cicalas crouched in ranks:
   Slack the thistle-head piled its down-silk grey:
Scarce the stony lizard sucked hollows in his flanks:
   Thick on spots of umbrage our drowsed flocks lay.
Sudden bowed the chestnuts beneath a wind un-
      heard,
   Lengthened ran the grasses, the sky grew slate:

George Meredith

Then amid a swift flight of winged seed white as
    curd,
  Clear of limb a Youth smote the master's gate.
      God! of whom music
      And song and blood are pure,
      The day is never darkened
      That had thee here obscure.

One may say those last words of Meredith's
own poetry. Often the God is obscure in it;
but we know that he has visited the poet; who
is labouring to tell us new and wonderful things
which the God has told him.

But all this fulness and sharpness of detail
threatens the end, as it marks the climax, of
the pure romantic poetry. It is the first sign
of that plethora of thought which, as Words-
worth said, would have prevented Shakespeare
from writing an epic. If all conditions had
favoured, Meredith might perhaps have made
the new poetry for which he prepared the
way. He might have kept the folk-song music
and enriched it with a more intellectual and
questioning emotion. As it was, the folk-song
music was often lost though he worked on
a folk-song basis. Sometimes, as in his Odes,
he followed the literary and Latin tradition of
English poetry; and he began the ode called
Youth in Memory with a passage that seems
intended to imitate the youthful poetry of his

friend Swinburne, and in that imitation to
symbolize youth itself:—

> Days, when the ball of our vision
> Had eagles that flew unabashed to sun ;
> When the grasp on the bow was decision,
> And arrow and hand and eye were one ;
> When the Pleasures, like waves to a swimmer,
> Came heaving for rapture ahead !—
> Invoke them, they dwindle, they glimmer
> As lights over mounds of the dead.

But notice, even here, how he disturbs the
metre with an unexpected foot in the second
and fourth lines. He cannot be content, like
Swinburne, just to glorify a familiar tune.
And so in his ballads and other poems with
a folk-song basis he cannot be content with a
folk-song simplicity of movement and thought.
The movement is constantly broken by com-
pression of the sense ; it is often rather a
précis of poetry than poetry itself. There is
an emphasis on each word because each has
to do the work of two or three. This is not
a solution of the problem which he set himself, of combining action and passion with
intellectual comment; for though the comment
is so much compressed that it does not swamp
the action and passion, the process of com-
pression jars the rhythm which is the proper

George Meredith

poetic expression of action and passion. Often we are only tantalized by the ballad form which leads us to expect a music we never get. In the metre itself we feel the poet's mind labouring after a primitive simplicity, for which it will not forgo any of its own modern activities. Therefore the labour is desperate and interests us in its process rather than delights us with its result. The ballads of tragic life are notes upon tragic situations forced into verse. They are wonderful, like Aristotle's *Ethics*; but they have little more music than that work has eloquence.

Often Meredith used the ballad form with a kind of irony, just as he used the eloquence of Shakespeare's sonnets ironically in *Modern Love*. In The Young Princess he begins:—

> When the South sang like a nightingale
> Above a bower in May,
> The training of Love's vine of flame
> Was writ in laws, for lord and dame
> To say their yea and nay.

You expect a simple story of romance and rapture; but all that follows is grim and complicated, and the burden is there like "La donna e mobile" in *Rigoletto*, only to make it grimmer by contrast. Often in his ballads

43

More Essays on Books

Meredith imitates rather the doggerel of debased ballad verse than the lyrical beauty of true folk-song. He is nearer to the latter than to the earlier version of *Chevy Chase*, not of course from failure of art, but by deliberate design. For in these ballads he cannot forbear to criticize the romantic standards which we associate with the ballad, and against which he reacts in all his poetry. And this criticism is apt to express itself in a kind of doggerel which is a parody of the romantic methods of expression. A verse will begin with romantic mouthing, and end in doggerel as in this example from *Archduchess Anne* :—

> I am a man of many sins,
>   Who for one virtue die,
> Count Louis said.—They play at shins,
>   Who kick, was the reply.

Count Louis is not allowed to Byronize without a rebuke ; and Byron himself gets a rebuke in the little poem called Manfred :—

> Somewhere about his grinder teeth,
> He mouthed of thoughts that grilled beneath,
> And summoned Nature to her feud
> With bile and buskin attitude.

Meredith, in fact, is always using the primitive forms of poetry to test the matter of poetry,

44

George Meredith

as if any spurious matter must betray itself at
once in forms so simple; and when it does
betray itself he derides it in doggerel.

But he is just as suspicious of spurious
matter when he writes in the literary tradition,
and this suspicion expresses itself in form no
less than in sense. He writes odes in irregular
verse like Cowley, but for a reason the very
opposite. Cowley hoped by his irregularities
to suggest a frenzy that could not be kept
within bounds. Meredith needed a form of
verse as near to prose as possible but without
the diffuseness of blank verse, so that he might
never be forced by his metre to seem more
poetic than he was. The *Meditation under
Stars* is indeed meditation for the most part,
and the labouring thought of the writer expresses itself in the broken lines that are so
near to intense and compressed prose. Only
when at the end emotion masters him do the
verses move swiftly and freely and the words
sing together in a common music :—

We behold

The love that lends her grace
Among the starry fold.
Then at new flood of customary morn,
Look at her through her showers,
Her mists, her streaming gold,
A wonder edges the familiar face;

She wears no more that robe of printed hours ;
Half strange seems Earth, and sweeter than her
    flowers.

In all Meredith's metres there is a clear and
candid expression of the process, poetic or half-
poetic, of his mind. He may irritate you, but
he will never beguile you into thinking that
he feels more than he does. He is for ever
trying to enrich the material of poetry, and
when he fails we know it at once from the
dissonance of his verse. But in that very dissonance he may be preparing for a future and
more subtle harmony, when some poet shall be
able to feel his ideas more instinctively than he
felt them and so to find an easier expression for
them ; and it may be that we, as we grow more
familiar with his sense, shall find an unexpected
music in his verse, even in the later odes on
French history ; for beauty often seems ugliness
when the mind is bewildered by its strangeness.

The Scholar's Religion   ⊺   ⊺   ⊺

A MAN'S religion, if it be more than a game or a drug, must be in his business and take some of its character from his business. It is the application of the universal to the particular; and the universal is qualified by that particular to which it is applied. In his presidential address to the Classical Association, Professor Gilbert Murray took for his subject "Religio Grammatici," the religion of a man of letters. He tells us what that religion is and how it, and it alone, justifies the business of a man of letters, by which he means a scholar to whom literature is literature and not words or constructions or facts. "Man," he says, "is imprisoned in the external present; and what we call a man's religion is, to a great extent, the thing that offers him a secret and permanent means of escape from that prison, a breaking of the prison walls which leaves him standing, of course, still in the present, but in a present so enlarged and enfranchised that it

47

becomes not a prison but a free world." If you are a scholar without the scholar's religion, you are imprisoned in your external present, which happens to be the past to other men, just as a grocer without his religion is imprisoned among his groceries. You have no hold of the universal, but lose yourself among your particulars, words, constructions, facts. You are, in fact, " shoppy." It is religion that prevents men from being shoppy and makes the shop of one man valuable to another; for all men, who have religion, have it in common and recognize it in each other, though in each it has the character of his own business.

What, then, is the religion of the scholar? He is concerned with the past. That is why men who are imprisoned in their own external present think him a luxury and one that no man of sense can enjoy. They prefer bad, pretty actresses and pay them better. But to him the past is the past only by the accident of time. His religion makes it also the present to him. For what he seeks in the past, what by reason of his peculiar knowledge and accomplishment he is able to seek in it, is eternity; and he believes in eternity and makes other men believe in it because he seeks and finds it in the past. Behind the diversities of time and place, always changing and passing, there is this eternal *quod semper quod ubique quod ab omnibus*; and, but for the memory of man maintained in literature and art, each one of us might think it peculiar to himself, an accident that happened to him now and then, a by-product of his own lonely struggle for life. It is the business of the scholar to keep that memory fresh, to trace the eternal through time, so that we may recognize it in ourselves and have confidence in it. But to do this he needs his own craft; he must know a dead language well enough to distinguish between the thoughts in it that are dead and those that are alive; for language alone can tell us whether its thought is living or dead, whether it belongs to time or to eternity. So for the scholar the dead language must be alive, that he may judge its literature as others judge that of their own time. It must speak to him as living men speak to each other; and all the labour and pains needed to acquire this knowledge of a dead language are justified only if their aim is the tracing of the eternal through time. They are useless if, with them all, the scholar remains in a parish of the past, as many now remain in a parish of the present.

Without his religion the scholar has no

discrimination; the past is utterly the past
to him, and all of equal interest because it is
the past. He is imprisoned in his period and
subject to all its provincialities of time and
place. He respects its peculiar heresies as the
philistine respects his own, not knowing that
they are provincial. He is overawed by
antiquity, as most of us are by modernity, and
is the slave of a herd instinct when the herd
itself is all ghosts. For the herd instinct
works in Homer, in Dante, in Shakespeare,
and makes them unintelligible to those who
are possessed by the instinct of their own herd.
But the eternal in them is their freedom from
it; and it may be recognized all through the
ages by this freedom. It is what men now feel
and think and say when they are freed from
their own herd instinct, when they are not of
the parish or the tribe but of humanity.

There are of course instincts and appetites
common to all men; but, though common,
they are particular not universal; they do not
free us from our external present but imprison
us in it. The expression of them is always of
the moment, hand to mouth, subject to circumstance; for posterity it has only an historical
interest; it does not communicate anything
but fact. The essence of the eternal is that it

The Scholar's Religion

communicates emotion, that emotion which the
eternal itself has aroused in the author; and
only the eternal can thus communicate emotion
through all the change of circumstance. Its
quality is in the very medium of expression,
the words, the paint, the stone. You may
talk about the eternal but your theme will not
keep your language alive; it may be dead with
all your own egotism and particularity. It is
not the theme that gives life, but the experience
of life itself in terms of the universal. But let
us take a particular instance. Nausicaa is as
much alive for us as Tolstoy's Nataasha, and
for the same reason. Homer could not have
drawn Nausicaa nor Tolstoy Nataasha if they
had been interested egotistically in particular
young women. When you are so interested
you talk about your "girl," you use parochial
language, or escape from it into poetical
formulæ. What is expressed in Nausicaa and
Nataasha is an interest, passionate because
religious rather than sexual, in all young girls.
They are part of the beauty of life itself; their
pretty ways are a gift from God to mankind,
like the spring and its flowers. Homer and
Tolstoy looked at them, and saw so much of
them, because they rejoiced universally and not
with any particular object of their own. They

were onlookers who saw most of the game; for they were not themselves playing it for victory. And we know this about Homer, though we may not know that he existed, because of the very quality of his words, because of the life in them which is the eternal.

There is this eternal quality to be found in the literature and art of all peoples; but you need discrimination to find it, to separate it from the dullness of circumstance; and some literature and art has it more constantly, more securely, than other. Some has inspired the world and increased its spiritual momentum, while other has to be discovered by experts in its own forgotten backwater of the past. And the experts who discover it, especially if it be of their own race, are apt to overrate it, to find some peculiar magic in it, as Freeman did in everything Anglo-Saxon, as Wagner did in the Niebelungenlied. There is room, says Professor Murray, for these exaggerations "as protests, as experiments, as personal adventures, or as reactions against a dominant main stream." There is also this great value in them, that they may increase our knowledge of the eternal by giving us more examples of it. We recognize it all the more surely in the Greeks if we have found it elsewhere; and we learn to reject

what is dull and stale and particular in the
Greeks themselves. We know much more
about Greek sculpture now, because it is not
the only sculpture in the world for us. We
see the difference between the Throne of Venus
and the Laocoön, because we see what the
Throne of Venus has in common with the other
great sculpture of the world, and what the
Laocoön lacks. To understand the Greeks we
must free our minds of snobbery about them,
the snobbery of the scholar or the connoisseur;
their eternal is hidden from those who would
make it a private possession of their own. But
there is more of the eternal in their art than
in any other for this reason, that in it they
think and feel simultaneously. They were the
first to pour all the eager activity of the brain
into art and literature; they would not refuse
to think so that they might act; and they
proved to all the world in art, in politics, in
every detail of life, that men act better for
thinking. But for their example, the whole
Western world might never have passed beyond
folk-song and proverbs and ballads, might
never have attained to the forms of great art.
Their eternity is larger and richer than that of
other peoples because there is in it the eternity
of ideas. Plato lived long after Homer, but

he was implied in the large forms of Homer and in his richness of content. His very conception of beauty lived, before he expressed it, in Greek art; for the artists had acted in terms of his thought; beauty had been to them something universal, serious, perceived with the whole mind and made by all its activities. The Greek drama welcomed all thought, and was enlarged and diversified in form by it; and all the great art of the modern world has attained to its own large and diverse forms because we have learnt from the Greeks this fusion of thought and emotion. Folk-song is good, but *The Magic Flute* is better, because it has the cumulative power of an idea running through all its songs, so that the beauty of it grows the deeper we are drawn into it. Mozart himself, though he knew nothing of the Greeks, lived in a world that had inherited them and their eternity and was of it.

But we have inherited that world through the labour of scholars. Browning in his Grammarian's Funeral seems not to do them full justice, for they laboured at the parts of speech, not for their own sake, but so that they might learn how to think. They knew that the eternity of thought was hidden in that language. The key to the universal

was in its very words, words chosen or made by
the first men who passed from feeling the
universal to thinking of it and naming it, and
who preserved the concept of it in language.
To regain that concept it was necessary to
know their language, and the grammarians,
scenting the universal, learnt it, and with it
the power of thought. They gave us not only
philosophy but possibilities of art which but
for philosophy would never be dreamed of,
and we are still unaware what we owe to
them.

Professor Murray deals with the common
belief that scholarship is hostile to progress.
There is a fear, he says, that "in studying the
great teachers of the past we are in some sense
wantonly sitting at the feet of savages"; and,
he continues, "there are in life two elements,
one transitory and progressive, the other com-
paratively, if not absolutely, non-progressive
and eternal, and the soul of man is chiefly
concerned with the second." True, the soul of
man is concerned with this eternal as a reality,
not ourselves, into which we can enter. Because
it is eternal and universal we cannot improve
it; we can only experience it and so become
a part of it, and our true business in life is to
become a part of it. As for material progress,

55

as for evolution itself, what is it but the freeing of our capacity for the eternal? Increase of power over the material world does not give us new faculties; it only allows us to exercise faculties hitherto latent. It is part of that whole process of evolution which is the giving of opportunity, to be used or wasted. This giving of opportunity is the progressive, transitory element in life; that for which opportunity is given is the eternal. So the individual may get or make his opportunity; and his capacity for the eternal may be suddenly and marvellously freed; and this may happen also to a whole people, as it happened to the Greeks. Then there is progress, which to the fool seems merely material, and which is transitory. But what, in that moment of freedom, is experienced and expressed is the eternal, is that which all other men will experience and express if they get the opportunity and use it. And those who do get it and use it recognize this eternal in the past, know that it is not their own invention but a discovery made now, made before, and to be made again and again. They know the accents of those who have discovered it, through all changes of circumstance, and the accents of those who have not. It is, Augustine said, "a beauty old as new," with the freshness and perpetual recurrence of the sunrise, and the scholar is he who is aware of . both.

So, as Professor Murray says, communion with the past and its discoverers of the eternal is a real fact. "The student, as he realizes it, feels himself one of a long line of torch-bearers. He attains to that which is the most compelling desire of every human being, a work in life which is worth living for, and which is not cut short by the accident of his own death." So we can reconcile what seem to be the contradictories of scholarship. The scholar receives the torch and hands it on; that is mere rhetoric, until you see that the torch is living fire. And the handing on of it is not only learning but doing. What we need in all education concerned with the eternal is to make the pupil feel that he is not only a learner but also a discoverer. If he reads a Greek play, it is not merely to master a text; it is to discover that which the writer had discovered, that beauty new as old; and the greater the number of those who discover it, the more secure are mankind in their possession of it. For each individual who discovers it does, with his own identity, discover something fresh in it, and may hand this on to others. The eternal is also infinite; nothing that is once said truly about it can ever be merely repeated; each experience of it is new because it is the experience of a new mind, though that which is experienced is always the same. We ourselves may be humble creatures, but, if once in our lives we experience the eternal, we add to the everlasting freshness of mankind. And this fact brings Professor Murray from a statement of the religion of the scholar to a statement of the religion of democracy. "The cardinal doctrine of that religion is the right of every human soul to enter, unhindered except by the limitation of its own powers and desires, into the full spiritual heritage of the race."

Scholars who pride themselves on their learning, as something of which the mass of men are incapable, are traitors to scholarship and prove that they are ignorant of its very subject-matter. To be proud of scholarship is to think that you have made the eternal your own private possession, which means that you have never experienced it. For those who have experienced it know that it is for all men, and long that all may possess it. That is why men become artists and philosophers; they wish all to share that which they have seen;

The Scholar's Religion

the wish is a necessary consequence of the
vision, for the vision itself is not complete
until it is shared. And so it is with the true
teacher, he is a teacher because, like the artist
and philosopher, he wishes to share what he
has seen; if he has seen it, he must wish to
share it. Fellowship is a quality of the
eternal; and to see it fills men with the desire
for fellowship. Recognize the accents of the
eternal in some poet of the past and you must
wish others to hear them. You have entered
into fellowship with that poet; and the two of
you, gathered together, wish all mankind to be
of your company. That was why he wrote;
that is why we praise him; that is why
Professor Murray translates Euripides.

Light and Humorous Verse ᔈ ᔈ

MOST anthologies have this defect, that
they are too large and therefore their
standard is not high.   Mediocre verse is even
less tolerable when it tries to be light or
humorous than when it tries to be passionate.
Mr. and Mrs. Melville, in their Anthology of
Humorous Verse, do well enough in their
earlier periods, where time has acted as critic
for them. They print a good many poems
that deserve to be better known than they are.
There is also an historic interest in ancient
attempts at humour even when they are not
humorous.   But this interest is lacking to the
failures of the nineteenth century, and the last
half of their book is full of these.   Indeed, it
reminds one of a curiosity shop full of shabby
Victorian furniture. Thus Theodore Hook's
verses about punning are neither new nor old ;
they are merely obsolete.

For instance, *ale* may make you *ail*, your *aunt* an
ant may kill.

You in a *vale* may buy a *veil*, and *Bill* may pay
the *bill*.

Light and Humorous Verse

Or if to France your *bark* you steer, at Dover, it
    may be,
A *peer* appears upon the *pier* who, blind, still goes
    to *sea*.

Somewhere in Germany there is a museum of
bad art, which no doubt has its uses; and it
appears from the preface that this book is
meant to be a kind of museum of humorous
verse. The authors tell us that they do not
put it forward as a collection of masterpieces;
their object has been " not only to bring together the best humorous verse in the language
between Robert Herrick and Owen Seaman,
but also to give representative specimens of
the work of those writers whose efforts were
acclaimed as successful by their contemporaries." Can anyone have ever been amused
by the lines I have quoted? If so, the fact
is historically interesting, but I should like
to see it proved. However, the collection has
evidently been made with great industry; and
those who have a taste for curiosities may even
like to look at the verses of Theodore Hook.

Mr. Leonard's anthology maintains a higher
standard, but I wish it were higher still.
" None can dispute," he says, " that in light
verse there is an extraordinary amount of
imperishable poetry which glorifies the English

language." Well, I dispute it, and not from
mere perversity. Indeed, I have often been
surprised at the small amount of good light
verse that has been written in any language—
that is to say, of light verse that is also poetry.
Mr. Leonard has sought far and wide, but
besides including many pieces that are not very
good he has left out a few that are. He gives us
Skelton's *Merry Margaret*, which is good enough,
but it is not so good or so light as the poem to
Mistress Isabel Pennell, which rises with such
natural art from the doggerel of the first verse—

> By Saint Mary, my lady,
> Your mammy and your daddy
> Brought forth a goodly baby,

to the poetry, enchanting though still close to
common speech, of the close—

> It were an heavenly health,
> It were an endless wealth,
> A life for God himself,
> To hear this nightingale
> Among the birdés small
> Warbling in the vale.

There is the same rise without discord or incongruity in Marvell's lines *To his Coy Mistress*,
and they too are omitted. Indeed, there is
nothing by Marvell in the book. By Thackeray
there are ten pieces, some of which have grown

stale; but we miss the lines on Mrs. Katherine's
Lantern, which will never grow stale. Yet one
cannot read any anthology without being surprised at its omissions; and Mr. Leonard has
included many poems for which we are grateful,
as, for instance, Jordan's Careless Gallant, though
he has "modified" certain lines which are not
very shocking in the original.

These two anthologies warn us that there is
a distinction to be drawn between light and
humorous verse, though the same poem may be
both, and though the terms are loosely used.
The best light verse is poetry at play, and
only a poet can write it.

What I speak, my fair Chloe, and what I write,
    shows
  The Difference there is betwixt Nature and Art:
I court others in Verse; but I love Thee in Prose:
  And They have my Whimsies; but Thou hast my
    Heart.

This is a light verse of a prosaic age and of a
worldly poet, yet it seems to be trembling into
poetry, and there is no incongruity in the
seriousness of the last word. Just as in the
light music of Mozart there is always a way
open towards passion, so it is with the light
verse of the masters; and in both it is beauty
of form that provides the opening. Good light

verse has the beauty of poetry and remembers poetry with respect. The versifier may laugh at himself, but he does not laugh at his art; and for that reason he does not laugh at all that his art implies. In his mood of the moment he may regard himself and another as butterflies hovering for a day over the flowers of an enchanted garden; but his object, like Watteau's, is to give an immortal rendering of that transient delight, and to connect it with eternity by an expression of his own sense of its transience. For, if we know that the moment is short, we know that the ages are long; and if we call ourselves trifles, we imply that there is a reality not trifling.

> But at my back I always hear
> Time's wingèd chariot hurrying near,
> And yonder all before us lie
> Deserts of vast eternity.

You cannot make poetry or anything else out of an entire disbelief; and when a poet seems to smile at himself and his passion in light verse, he smiles really at the incongruity between his own little momentary self and the great eternal passion that has entered into it.

Light verse always has the instability of moods. In it the poet does not laugh at high sustained flights, but confesses himself unequal

to them. He confesses himself to be less than
what he wishes to say; therefore he will only
hint at it, smiling at his own impotence of
expression.

> What is this? *Ma foi*, the fact is
> That my hand is out of practice,
> And my poor old fiddle cracked is,
> And a man—I let the truth out—
> Who's had almost every tooth out,
> Cannot sing as once he sung,
> When he was young as you are young,
> When he was young and lutes were strung,
> And love lamps in the casement hung.

To see the difference between light and humorous verse we have only to contrast Marvell's
Coy Mistress, from which we have quoted
the most famous lines, with his satires—for
instance, with this passage from The Character of Holland :—

> Glad then, as miners that have found the ore,
> They with mad labour fished the land to shore,
> And dived as desperately for each piece
> Of earth, as if 't had been of ambergris,
> Collecting anxiously small loads of clay,
> Less than what building swallows bear away,
> Or than those pills which sordid beetles roll,
> Transfusing into them their dunghill soul.

Marvell was a poet, and never quite at his ease
in utterly prosaic verse. But the point to be
noted is that he tries to make the verse here

E
65

utterly prosaic, as he tries to make it humorous.
For whereas light verse is poetry at play,
humorous verse is usually prose at play, and
can be made by men who are not poets at all
and could not write a line with the music of
poetry in it. Good humorous verse, though it
takes the form of poetry, keeps the peculiar
virtues of prose. Take, for instance, the famous
lines from *Hudibras*, in which the Puritans
are said to

> Compound for sins they are inclined to,
> By damning those they have no mind to :
> Still so perverse and opposite
> As if they worshipped God for Spite.

These are to be admired for their intellectual,
not for their emotional, qualities. They are
verse only because Butler was not serious
enough to write prose. He laughs at Hudibras
and advertises his laughter in his form. For
there is an incongruity between the form
proper to the expression of emotion and the
purely prosaic virtue of the matter, which
makes us laugh independently of the matter
itself, and it is this incongruity which sometimes causes verse to be unintentionally humorous, as in an unsuccessful Newdigate poem upon
the Pilgrim Fathers, in which this couplet
occurs—

Light and Humorous Verse

So, ever guided by the hand of God,
They sailed along until they reached Cape Cod.

Here we have prose masquerading as verse
without knowing it, but in Swift and Butler it
masquerades intentionally and profits by the
greater brevity which the form of verse imposes
upon it, and by the fact that the form advertises
its humorous intention; for we assume that a
writer means to be humorous when he puts
prosaic matter into a poetic form.

Unfortunately this assumption, so easily
induced, has led many writers to think that
humorous verse is easily made. Mr. and Mrs
Melville's anthology contains many pieces which
have nothing to recommend them except the
incongruity between matter and form. Here,
for instance, are the first two lines of A Vision
of Siren Soup, by Shirley Brooks :—

The alderman woke from his nightmare, howling a
    terrible cry ;
Punched his wife's face with his elbow; at morning
    she had a black eye.

The rest is no better, and it has only one object,
namely, to advertise the fact that it is meant
to be humorous. It reminds one of the
comedian who paints his nose red to show that
he is funny and then has nothing funny to say.
Anyone can see now that it is not good, for

its style is quite out of fashion. But much of
our modern humorous verse will seem no better
when it also goes out of fashion; for it is still
not commonly understood that verse is not
worth writing at all unless it has the virtues
either of poetry or of prose. The incongruity
between matter and form is not enough to
justify its existence. We have many writers
who say nothing in their verses except that
they are not poets and do not wish to be.
They use verse as a means of laughing at
poetry, not at themselves. They parody
emotions when they are not parodying styles,
and they do so merely to raise a laugh and
without any reserve of admiration. All parody
is a parasitic form of art, and it is often a
troublesome parasite. Mr. Leonard in his
notes quotes Swinburne's outburst against
Calverley, " A jester, graduate or under-
graduate, may be fit enough to hop, skip, and
tumble before University audiences, without
capacity to claim an enduring or even a passing
station among even the humblest of English
humourists." This may seem harsh; but Swinburne was provoked by the fact that Calverley
taught his imitators a fatally easy way of rais-
ing a laugh and that he himself had often no
object except to raise one as easily as he could.

Light and Humorous Verse

Calverley's defect is poverty of subject-matter. He wrote for a small class, not for the world; and he wrote about things that are amusing only to that class. His parodies, unlike Swinburne's, are criticisms of the manner of the poet parodied, not of his mind. They are more amusing than just, mere practical jokes brilliantly executed, whereas Swinburne's parody of Mrs. Browning is a *reductio ad absurdum*, and we feel that Mrs. Browning herself might have written it in an unguarded moment. Parody is caricature; and like the best caricatures, the best parodies have an essential, not merely an accidental, likeness to the original. They are concerned with its very nature, not with its mannerisms. Here, for instance, is a verse from Swinburne's parody of Mrs. Browning in which the Woodlouse justifies itself to the Poet :—

And I sacrifice, a Levite—and I palpitate, a poet;
Can I close dead ears against the rush and
    resonance of things?
Symbols in me breathe and flicker up the heights
    of the heroic;
Earth's worst spawn, you said, and cursed me?
    look ! approve me ! I have wings.

That has even some of the merits of the victim, and could only have been written by one who had read her with delight. There is only one of Swinburne's parodies which is an attack upon the writer parodied, and that is a long dull failure.

But parody at best is a trivial kind of humorous poetry. It only ceases to be trivial when it is practised incidentally, as by Aristophanes, and with some larger purpose. The parodist has his material provided for him, and if it is a well-known poem he is sure to make some one laugh. But in other kinds of humorous poetry the writer has to provide his own material; and he must be judged by the quality of that as well as of his execution. Hood, for all his ingenuity, is becoming obsolete because his material is usually poor. He makes verbal jokes round a subject-matter not humorous. But the *Ingoldsby Legends* are still good to read because their subject-matter is humorous, and the *Bab Ballads* are likely to last for the same reason; there are sound prosaic merits in both. Like Barham, Sir William Gilbert had usually a good story to tell; like Barham, too, he had an original mastery of comic verse, and could laugh in it as the poets sing in poetry. Of the two Barham was superior in energy and Gilbert in idea. It was Barham's peculiar gift to combine a headlong volubility of speech with a mechanical perfection of versification so as to make us laugh at their incongruity. This was not a mere trick, for his high spirits were real, not affected for literary purposes, and he seems to write in verse rather than in prose for the same reason that a child dances when it might walk. Gilbert also had high spirits, but he had more satiric power than Barham. He thought more, and combined ideas with high · spirits as he combined extravagance with demureness. He could make prosaic sentences dance in verse as if they were solemn people mesmerized. Neither he nor Barham assumes a humorous manner; their fun seems to grow naturally out of their attitude towards life; they are like good actors whose art is being rather than acting. And that is the secret of all humorous verse. · You must be humorous before you can write it. No desire to ridicule things, no verbal dexterity, no trick of style, will give success. Unfortunately, the man who is not humorous by nature is the last to suspect his own deficiency.

A New Planet ◌ ◌ ◌ ◌ ◌

HAVING discovered Chinese painting, we are beginning to discover Chinese poetry. The process is slow, for it has to be performed for us by scholars; the poetry, unlike the pictures, must be translated for us. Yet it brings us not merely new knowledge, but also a new delight; for it is the peculiar virtue of Chinese poetry that it remains poetry in a literal translation. Something must be lost, but the more literal the translation the more we become aware of the merits of the original. It is a strange and wonderful experience to read Mr. Waley's translations of Chinese poetry. Read them and you will find that a new planet swims into your ken.

Mr. Waley says that any literal translation of Chinese poetry "is bound to be to some extent rhythmical, for the rhythm of the original obtrudes itself." Certainly there is a delicate rhythm in his translations, and this poetry seems to speak naturally to us in our own language, without any addition of English poetic ornament. So powerful is it that it makes poetry of English words that are only struggling to give the sense of it, and a poetry which, though new to us, seems to supply something that has always been wanting to the poetry of Europe.

It is the same with the versions, less literal perhaps and more literary, of Mr. Ezra Pound. He, too, astonishes us with a new beauty; we recognize it as we recognize a new and wonderful tune, and we wonder why no European poet has ever written thus. For there is nothing outlandish or primitive in it. Rather, it is more civilized than any poetry of our own, more reasonable and nearer to prose. The great poets of Europe, in their themes and their language, insist that they are poets. They start singing, as it were, with a magnificent gesture; but the Chinese poet starts talking in the most ordinary language and voice of the most ordinary things; and his poetry seems to happen suddenly out of the commonplace, as if it were a beautiful action happening in the routine of actual life. That, no doubt, is why it suffers so little in a literal translation. Its beauty is the beauty of thought itself; and the poet does not try to raise himself to beauty of thought by beauty of language. He practises no auto-suggestion, and is concerned less with his own feelings than with what has stirred them. European poetry is apt to express merely feelings and to express them in the music of words. So often, without that music, it is nothing. But Chinese poetry gives us the very cause of emotion, which arouses that emotion in the reader even when expressed in the plainest words. Here, for instance, are some lines from a poem of the Han dynasty, written in the first century B.C., in which a poor man tells how he resolves to go out into the world to make his fortune, and how his wife tries to keep him at home :—

There was not a peck of rice in the bin ;
There was not a coat hanging on the pegs.
So I took my sword and went towards the gate.
My wife and child clutched at my coat and wept :
"Some people want to be rich and grand,
I only want to share my porridge with you.
Above we have the blue waves of the sky ;
Below the yellow face of this little child."

Here we are moved by what the wife says, and it has only to be said in the simplest words to move us, as if a great poet had written it in our own tongue. Something happens in the

poem; and it happens again in the translation. It is truth, the truth of the love
and nature of woman, a universal truth that
makes its own music; and all the poet has
done is to see it and tell us what he has
seen.

It is the peculiar art of Chinese poets not to
arouse any expectation in us by their method
of address. European poets have the ambition
to make an orchestra out of language; but
the Chinese seem to play on a penny whistle,
and then suddenly, with a shy smile, to draw
the most wonderful thin music out of it. Anyone could do it, they seem to say; and they
convince us that poetry is not a rare and exotic
luxury, but something that happens in life
itself, something that one needs only to watch
for and record. They are passive to this
poetry of reality; they take it in and then
give it out again, without insisting that it is
their own achievement, without wishing us to
be impressed with the momentousness of their
passions or the depth of their sorrows. And
for them there is no class of poetic events;
they are the most utter realists, but not on
principle or in any reaction from the
romantic. Nothing is common or unclean to
them, and they have the innocence of

Paradise with the sensitiveness of an old and exquisite civilization. They have ideas; but ideas have not made them blind to things; rather they see things more vividly in the light of ideas. Like Mozart, they give us the folk-song of a philosopher.

Again and again one is struck by the beautiful manners of these poets, manners which make them more, and not less, poetic. Both the T'ang and the pre-T'ang poetry seem to belong to an age of reason, but reason controls rather than chills their passion. It is the poetry of the sober who need no incitement of the appetites and no mob-contagion to put them in love with life. Their love-poems are written rather to wives and children than to mistresses; and they combine the politeness of Prior with the tenderness of a ballad. Here is a passage from a poem of farewell which Ch'in Chia, a poet of the Han dynasty, sends to his wife, because she is ill and away from home and he cannot see her before going to the capital to take up an appointment :—

One parting but ten thousand regrets;
As I take my seat my heart is unquiet.
What shall I do to tell you all my thoughts?
How shall I let you know of all my love?

A New Planet

Precious hairpins make the head to shine,
And bright mirrors can reflect beauty.
Fragrant herbs banish evil smells,
And the scholar's harp has a clear note.
The man in the book of odes who was given a
  quince
Wanted to pay it back with diamonds and rubies.
When I think of all the things you have done for
  me,
How ashamed I am to have done so little for you.
Although I know that it is a poor return,
All I can give you is this description of my
  feelings.

And here is a poem which Po Chu-i sends, while on a journey, to his little daughter A-Kuei, whom he has left with her nurse, Mrs. Ts'ao :—

To distant service my heart is well accustomed ;
When I left home it wasn't that which was difficult,
But because I had to leave Miss Ku'ei at home—
For this it was that tears filled my eyes.
Little girls ought to be daintily fed :
Mrs. Ts'ao, please see to this.
That's why I've packed and sent a silver spoon.
You will think of me and eat up your food nicely.

Our poets seem often to be looking away out of their own lives into some distance of the past. Po Chu-i finds all his wonder in his own life ; it is on the ground he treads and not in the blue far-away mountains, and it is in the language, the images, of ordinary life. Yet it is never prosaic in the bad sense, never subdued to the routine of life or ill-natured with mere discontent. He and the other Chinese poets do not complain of the world that it is stupid and hostile. Their business is to surprise the beauty of the world and to be surprised by it. They are like good craftsmen who make lovely things out of objects of use by shaping them, not by ornament. And there is for them a likeness, not a romantic contrast, between human life and the beauty of nature. Po Chu-i, being on duty all night in the palace, dreams thus of a temple in the mountains :—

At the western window I paused from writing
    rescripts ;
The pines and bamboos were all buried in stillness.
The moon rose and a calm wind came ;
Suddenly, it was like an evening in the hills.
And so, as I dozed, I dreamed of the south-west
And thought I was staying at the Hsien-yu Temple.
When I woke and heard the dripping of the palace.
    clock
I still thought it was the murmur of a mountain
    stream.

And these poets have that delight in places which is the surest sign of a happy society. The place, the people, the season, are all a

A New Planet

part of the music of this poem by an emperor
of the sixth century A.D. :—

A beautiful place is the town of Lo–Yang ;
The big streets are full of spring-light.
The lads go driving out with harps in their hands :
The mulberry girls go out to the fields with
    their baskets.
Golden whips glint at the horses' flanks,
Gauze sleeves brush the green boughs.
Racing dawn, the carriages come home,
And the girls with their high baskets full of fruit.

Though far away in time and space, this Lo-
Yang is like an old West-country town where
the people know how to be happy in the
orchards close to their streets, where the spring
blossom is in their hearts and their voices, and
they have no desire to be what they are not.
These poets have not that desire which makes
us and our poetry ugly and restless.   For them
beauty is in things as they are and their business is to find it, beauty in all the simple things
that happen to men, not in the peculiar misunderstood passions of poets.   And the beauty
they find is so quiet, so reasonable, so irresistible, like the actions of a saint, that the more
we know of it the more it must affect our own
poetry, which is now expectant of a future it
has not yet found.   The poetry of our own
great past seems to be worked, out, both in

language and in themes. The young poets of
the present do not experiment merely for the
sake of the game, but because they are trying
to find poetic manners and moods natural to
themselves and their own time and circumstances. They are not content to sink into
mere prose, to make a literature like our manu-
facturing towns; nor to pretend to be Miltons
and Shelleys and Swinburnes, as the Roman
poets of the decadence pretended to be Virgils.
So, as Europe at the Renaissance found its
own future in the literature of ancient Greece,
our poets may now find their future in the
poetry of ancient China; they may recognize
in it that which they themselves wish to do.
This recognition would not be the imitation of
a barren age at the mercy of its own past.
The Chinese poetry moves us because it seems
to be not of yesterday but of to-morrow. Here
are the values, at once simple and subtle and
clear, that we desire. It is the poetry of men
who know what they want in life and who
want what is worth having for all men and not
for peasants alone or dilettantes or blond
monsters or archaic saints. It is the poetry
and the language and the desire of all men;
it is the universal that is in us all, men, women,
and children; and we do not need to force

ourselves into some unnatural state of mind to
enjoy it. One could quote these poems any-
where and to anyone, in the midst of conversa-
tion, without change of voice and without any
sense of incongruity; for to the Chinese poet
there are no incongruities and no separation of
poetry and prose in life. All life trembles into
beauty like leaves stirred by the wind; and it
remains itself even while it trembles.

There are many things in Taoism that we
cannot understand; but perhaps the Chinese
poets will help us to understand them. For
they seem to have by nature that passive
attitude to reality, "beyond good and evil,"
which Taoism aims at. "The perfect man
employs his mind as a mirror. It grasps
nothing; it refuses nothing. It receives, but
does not keep." The Chinese poet seems to
receive everything and to keep nothing. In
his passivity he takes in and he gives out, as if
his art were a process of nature, as if he were
a plant absorbing the sunlight and pouring
it out again in scent. He does not seem to
choose even his themes; they also happen to
him, and he cannot write of what does not
happen to him. But Western poets have
always been too wilful; they have been resolved
to make this or that happen to them; and so

they have a class of poetic themes and also a poetic language. But, for the Chinese, poetry is something beyond language. As Chuang Tzu, the Taoist philosopher, says: " The *raison d'être* of a fish trap is the fish. When the fish is caught, the trap may be ignored. The *raison d'être* of language is idea. When the idea is expressed, the language may be ignored." And Chinese poetry has a strange power of making us ignore language, as if the pure idea happened to us when we read it. It produces in us that utter passivity of which the Taoists speak, so that our minds make no resistance to it. There is no egotism in the poet to provoke our own, not even the egotism that lusts after fine execution. The Chinese poet does not, like Keats, look on fine phrases like a lover. There is never any emphasis in his poetry; never at any one point does anything happen. But the whole poem happens, to us as it has happened to him: and only when you have finished it do you see how completely it has happened. As the Chinese say, in poetry the sense goes on when the sound has ceased. You become a poet yourself as you read it; an experience has been communicated to you so that it is your own, so that you have lived it, and not merely read it; and, as for the words,

82

they are forgotten in the fact. So to read
this poetry gives you a disgust for the outworn
professionalism of our poets. It sets you on
your guard against their very methods of
address; they seem like stump orators after one
has been listening to quiet and exquisite talk.
And they themselves know this; they are ill at
ease in the trappings of the past, tired of fancy
dress; they wish to speak like ordinary men,
and yet to remain poets.

The Defects of English Prose ✧ ✧

I CANNOT read Mr. Pearsall Smith's anthology of English Prose without thinking of the anthology I would make myself and wondering all the while why his differs from mine. Why, among writers of the past, does he omit Shaftesbury and give but one passage from Johnson, when he gives so many from Sir Thomas Browne? Why is there not more of Gibbon's wit, and why not his great passage upon the funeral and character of Julian the Apostate? Why so many short, laboured, and not profound sentences from Carlyle followed by but one extract from Newman? Why the Gioconda passage from Pater, which has the defect that it is false? Why no Dickens at all, and no William Morris, and no W. H. Hudson? The answer is that Mr. Pearsall Smith lays his own emphasis in this anthology and I should lay another. For him our prose is greatest when it is nearest to poetry; it is overshadowed by our poetry

84

The Defects of English Prose

and almost its poor relation. A Frenchman reading his anthology might say: " All this is magnificent, but it is hardly prose. This is the literature of a people that can sing and preach, but cannot converse. I listen with amazement to all these prophets, but I should not care to talk with them; for, to tell the truth, they are not civilized. They do not seem to be men like myself, only abler; they are chiefs or elders at a tribal gathering, practising the eloquence of barbarians."

Yet there is another side to English prose which Mr. Pearsall Smith almost ignores: perhaps because he is making an anthology and that other side cannot easily be exhibited in extracts. Prose of its very nature is longer than verse, and the virtues peculiar to it manifest themselves gradually. If the cardinal virtue of poetry is love, the cardinal virtue of prose is justice; and, whereas love makes you act and speak on the spur of the moment, justice needs inquiry, patience, and a control even of the noblest passions. But English Prose, as Mr. Pearsall Smith presents it, is at the mercy of its passions and just only by accident. By justice here I do not mean justice only to particular people or ideas, but a habit of justice in all the processes of thought,

85

a style tranquillized and a form moulded by
that habit. The master of prose is not cold,
but he will not let any word or image inflame
him with a heat irrelevant to his purpose.
Unhasting, unresting, he pursues it, subduing
all the riches of his mind to it, rejecting all
beauties that are not germane to it; making
his own beauty out of the very accomplishment
of it, out of the whole work and its proportions,
so that you must read to the end before you
know that it is beautiful. But he has his
reward, for he is trusted and convinces, as
those who are at the mercy of their own
eloquence do not; and he gives a pleasure all
the greater for being hardly noticed. In the
best prose, whether narrative or argument, we
are so led on as we read, that we do not stop
to applaud the writer: nor do we stop to
question him. But we stop, whether to
applaud or to question, at a sentence such as
this, which Mr. Pearsall Smith gives us from
Carlyle—

Brave Sea captain, Norse Sea-king Columbus,
my hero, royalist Sea-king of all! it is no
friendly environment this of thine, in the waste
deep waters: round thee mutinous discouraged
souls, behind thee disgrace and ruin, before
thee the unpenetrated veil of Night.

The Defects of English Prose

If a writer continues long in this style, he wearies us like a man talking at the top of his voice ; and if he does not continue, the passage distracts us with its incongruity, like a sudden shouting. Carlyle here, and often, yields to a habit of excitement as if he had a right to be indulged in it. He is like a man who will make speeches at the dinner-table to show the force of his convictions. These are the manners of egotism, and egotism is the worst of all faults in prose.

For prose is the achievement of civilization, of people who have learned to discuss without blows or invective, who know that truth is hard to find and worth finding, who do not begin by accusing an opponent of wickedness, but elicit reason and patience by displaying them. You cannot say in poetry what the best prose says, or accomplish what the best prose accomplishes. Civilization may not surpass a primitive society in heights of rapture or heroism, but it is, if it be civilization, better for everyday life, kinder, more rational, more sustained in effort ; and this kindness and reason and sustained effort are expressed and encouraged in the masterpieces of prose. The French understood this long ago, because they prize civilization and enjoy it. Pascal, writing

his *Provincial Letters* in 1656 upon a subject
obscured by mediaeval subtleties and distorted
by party passions, is already just, polite, and
lucid; he does not even affect the magnificent
disdain of Gibbon, but is a civilized man talking to other civilized men, and therefore all the
more deadly in debate. But it is fallacies that
he would kill, not those who maintain them.
He knows that the art of controversy is, not to
begin with invective, but to state your case in
such a way that those who like invective will
supply it themselves against your adversary.

So we read Milton's controversy for its
accidents, splendid as they are, but Pascal's
still for the controversy itself. Though he is
not clothed in shining armour, he fights for the
children of light in all ages, with no pretence
of being an angel or a dervish, but quietly
appealing to the everlasting reason from whence
comes his help. In this book of Mr. Pearsall
Smith's, with its array of great names and
great passages, we notice how his moderns seem
to archaise when they would soar, as if they
must pretend to be of the giant race before
the flood so as to believe in their own greatness. Emerson says:—

Our friendships hurry to short and poor
conclusions, because we have made them a

texture of wine and dreams, instead of the tough fibre of the human heart.

Ruskin, even in *Praeterita*, writes thus of his first sight of the Alps:—

Infinitely beyond all that we had ever thought or dreamed—the seen walls of lost Eden could not have been more beautiful to us; not more awful round Heaven, the walls of sacred Death.

Pater begins a paragraph:—

I have remarked how in the process of our brain-building, as the house of thought in which we live gets itself together like some airy bird's nest of floating thistle-down and chance straws, compact at last, little accidents have their consequence.

Stevenson, in a letter, and talking of familiar things, says:—

Methought you asked me—frankly, was I happy? Happy (said I); I was happy only once; that was at Hyères; it came to an end from a variety of reasons, decline of health, change of place, increase of money, age with his stealing steps; since then, as before then, I know not what it means.

It is always finely, but not naturally, said.

Each writer seems to have a model not quite suited to the matter or the occasion, and makes us think of this model when we should be thinking only of what he has to say.

But the prose which interests us most, and persuades us unconsciously to go on reading it, seems to be made by the matter and the occasion; it is like talk between intimates, and the writer draws us into intimacy by his manner of address, which assumes that we do not wish to be tricked or dazzled, that, if he has anything worth saying, we shall listen to it for its own sake.

There is less of this prose in our literature than we could wish, but more than we should gather from Mr. Pearsall Smith's anthology. It began to be written about the time of the Restoration by Cowley, Halifax, and Dryden among others. Mr. Pearsall Smith gives one short passage from Cowley, one from Halifax, and none from Dryden—perhaps he thinks that the best of Dryden's prose is in his verse. But the first easy master of it is Shaftesbury, especially in his *Letter concerning Enthusiasm*. Here the case is all the more remarkable because he is talking of religion and saying things both novel and profound about it. His plea is for good humour in controversy, and he gives an example of it in his own letter. He begins lightly enough, and then, with a humane and natural art, leads us into seriousness:—

The Defects of English Prose

This, my Lord, is the security against super-
stition : To remember that there is nothing in
God but what is God-like ; and that He is
either not at all or truly and perfectly good.
But when we are afraid to use our reason freely,
even on that very question, " Whether He
really be, or not "; we then actually presume
Him bad, and flatly contradict that pretended
character of goodness and greatness, whilst we
discover this mistrust of His temper, and fear
His anger and resentment in the case of this
freedom of enquiry.

But though this is just and even now fresh, we
cannot deny that it lacks the music and images
of Jeremy Taylor or Milton ; and they are
absent from the prose of Johnson and all the
eighteenth century. For that reason the
Romantics despised even its virtues ; for them,
again, prose became the poor relation of poetry,
and must wear its cast-off clothes ; or else they
wrote like orators addressing a crowd with
repetitions and loud emphasis, abrupt transi-
tions and noisy images. Hazlitt is more
eloquent than scrupulous ; he never seems to
be alone with you as you read him, but rather
speaking to catch votes, even though it be for
the best writers or painters ; and Macaulay,
ignored by Mr. Pearsall Smith, is worse. His
prose has all the defects of a nation political

rather than social, he is incapable of meditation or even of converse, but lectures always; while Burke writes of the Sublime and Beautiful like an orator.

So, but for a few shy, never enough honoured writers, there is one whole province of the English mind left out of our prose, for we are capable of meditation and intimate talk; we are more civilized than our manners or our style. Mr. W. H. Hudson, for instance, seems always to be meditating or remembering; writing for him is a means of saying what he would never say aloud. He makes his dearest friend of the reader, and confides in him with speech that has the beauty of a wild animal's eyes. And Mark Rutherford, with a different kind of matter but the same shyness and melancholy faith, arouses a like confidence in us. These writers seldom say much in a single sentence or even paragraph, but they have a cumulative power that cannot be proved by quotation, a wandering music that blows where it lists, because they never force their inspiration or tell you what they have not got to say. Their peculiar quality is justice; they describe without a laboured eagerness or momentum, and without vivid words, just what they have seen and felt. They do not exploit their loves

The Defects of English Prose

or their hatreds, and it is wonderful that you should remember so well what is said with so little emphasis or apparent skill of words. Yet it is remembered, like a thought that does not need saying; it sinks deep into the mind, beyond language, like an actual experience, and, if you read their books with care, you are changed as if by an event.

But such writers are likely to remain few, for they are little encouraged. We are not yet a public of readers civilized enough to demand the highest virtues of prose; we prefer "clamorous sublimities" and phrases that ask to be noticed; we must be urged through a book by the crack of the writer's whip. Yet still one dreams of a prose that has never yet been written in English, though the language is made for it and there are minds not incapable of it, a prose dealing with the greatest things quietly and justly as men deal with them in their secret meditations, seeming perhaps to wander, but always advancing in an unbroken sequence of thought, with a controlled ardour of discovery and the natural beauties of a religious mind. Johnson might have written it, if he had had a stronger sense of beauty and more faith in the flights of reason; Newman if he had been a greater master of words and less afraid of his own questioning; Henry James if he had exercised his subtlety on larger things. But the best of our prose writers, living or dead, are not civilized enough, or too much in love with something else, or not enough in love with anything, to write the prose we dream of. The English Plato is still to be.

"God the Invisible King" ✑   ✑   ✑

IN men's conceptions of God, theology is
later than myth, and it has never been able
to control myth with its logic.   While the
philosopher tries to deduce all the logical im-
plications from the postulate God, it is the
common mind that clothes God with character,
that makes Him real and alive, and often, in
the process, makes Him undivine.   The problem
of the ages has been to conceive of a God who
is both real and divine, who has both logic and
life in Him ; and because all through the ages
logic has been sacrificed to life, or life to logic,
there have always been men, since there has
been theology, who refused to believe in a God
at all.   But often this refusal of theirs, though
it seems to them absolute, is really provisional.
All actual conceptions of God are either futile
in their own unreality or dangerous with the
egotism of man ; therefore it is wisest not even
to ask whether God exists.   But men will
not rest content with this provisional refusal ;

95

never will they despair of conceiving the real God and recognizing His reality in their conception; and in his book *God the Invisible King*, Mr. Wells makes the attempt once more.

His God is not an explanation of things. "There has always been a demand upon the theological teacher," he says, "that he should supply a cosmogony"; and in answer to that demand the unreal God is supplied, the Great First Cause. His God is not a Great First Cause; he insists that men, because they have thought of God as an explanation, have had a wrong conception of divinity; it has meant for them omnipotence, omniscience, infinity, the absolute, all mere theological abstractions. The real God must be freed from these and from the bondage of man's logic. He must be a person, finite, struggling, imperfect in all things except in intention. His divinity consists in His purity of intention, and in His immortality; and nothing distinguishes Him from other kinds of life except this immortality. In all other respects He, like the whole universe, is becoming. It is not merely creation that groaneth and travaileth; but also God Himself, who has not created it, who, though immortal, does not dwell in

eternity, but in time and space and change.
He is a part of the universe which groaneth
and travaileth, that part of it which means
well and only well. But He is not merely
something not ourselves, or ourselves, that
makes for righteousness. He is, Mr. Wells
insists, a person and a righteous person, One
whom we can admire and love, as we love and
admire each other. Like us at our best, He
means well, but, unlike us, He means always
and purely well. Besides and behind this God,
there is a "Veiled Being" whom we cannot
know or love or admire, and of whom God
Himself may know little more than we do.
The origin of God, for He seems to have had
an origin, is not known to Himself any more
than to us. All we can know is that He is,
that He is our Captain; and that our duty is
to make of the world a theocracy, so that we
may be all at one in doing His will.

But we must be perfectly disinterested in
our desire to do His will. He does not promise
to us, as individuals, eternal life. Indeed,
belief in Mr. Wells's God is incompatible with
belief in individual immortality, for His aim is
the conquest of death, "first the overcoming
of death in the individual by the incorporation
of the motives of his life into an undying pur-

pose, and then the defeat of that death that
seems to threaten our species upon a cooling
planet beneath a cooling sun." That is the
aim of God and of man; that is why man is to
be disinterested, and that is how he is to share
the disinterestedness of God. Both are to aim
at this overcoming of death, and the virtues of
man, as of God, are generated in this aim.

It is here that we become aware of the inadequacy of Mr. Wells's conception of God,
and of man. We are reminded of the question
which Morris asked about the Great Social
Revolution—" As we turn away from the flag-
staff where the new banner has been just run
up; as we depart, our ears yet ringing with
the blare of the heralds' trumpets that have
proclaimed the new order of things, what shall
we turn to then?" His answer is—Our daily
labour, freed at last from the tyranny of the
struggle for life. So, too, no doubt, Mr. Wells
would say, that in the conquest of death man
will achieve virtues, joys, faculties undreamt
of; and these he will still experience and
exercise when he has conquered death. Yes!
but, according to Mr. Wells's conception of
man and God, of the whole universe, all virtues,
all joys, all faculties are evolved in this process
of the conquest of death; it is a biological

conception, and has the defect of all biological
conceptions when they are applied to our
values, that, for it, everything is provisional,
everything is valued in terms of something else
—namely, the conquest of death, which is not
a positive good, but the removal of an evil.
Since all that is good is evolved in the effort
to remove that evil, all good exists in relation
to that evil; and what will become of the good
when the evil is removed ?

The mind of man can never be content with
this provisional valuing of things; for it is
passionately convinced that our values are not
all thus provisional. When we love, we love
things themselves and not their tendencies.
Our interest in their tendencies is scientific and
moral; but in love there is another quality,
which must be also in the love of God, if God
is to be real to us; and that is the quality
which man expresses in his art. It is the
essence of love that it is not provisional; if we
discover it to be provisional it is no longer
love for us. Love affirms passionately that it
is for the object in itself; and art expresses
this affirmation. Now it is interesting to find
Mr. Wells, in this book, describing art as " an
exploration of inherent human possibility ";
as, in fact, a kind of science. But art is not a

kind of science; the scientific element in it is
only a means to its own end, which is the
expression of man's values. Mr. Wells, when
he is most an artist, is not even indirectly concerned with the conquest of death; he expresses
values for men and women in themselves, and
his art has for us a value in itself and not in
the remotest relation to the conquest of death.
This immediate value, this love, enters into all
religion, is the essence of religion, which is
indeed the affirmation of absolute values, and,
when it becomes fully conscious, of the absolute
value of God.

But Mr. Wells, aiming at a conscious religion,
at the discovery of a real God, still thinks in
terms of the struggle for life. His object is to
harmonize that struggle with religion, to ex-
plain the existence of God in terms of it. He
would reconcile our values with the struggle
for life by insisting that God Himself takes
part in it, and that God is to be valued because
He takes part in it. His virtue consists in the
fact that He is trying to conquer death for us;
and our virtue is the effort to conquer death.
In that effort we do conquer death in so far
that we cease to fear it; and, being thus freed
from the fear of death, we attain to salvation.
Morally perhaps this view is adequate; but

man, at his best, is not a merely moral being;
and he cannot be content with a God who is
merely moral, as he is not content with men
who are merely moral. Just as we love men
for what they are and not only for what they
are trying to do, so we must love God for what
He is and not only for what He is trying to
do. God, for those who are most intensely
aware of Him, is an artist as well as a philanthropist; but Mr. Wells's God is only a
philanthropist. He has but one function,
namely, to conquer death for man.

Those who believe in Mr. Wells's God will
thus cut themselves off from some of the
avenues by which men have actually and most
intensely experienced God. For the sense of
God has poured into men, not merely through
their own efforts or the efforts of other men,
but through the achieved beauty of the universe; and that beauty has been to them, not
effort to be valued merely for what it is trying
to be or to do, but the expression of a state of
being beyond all effort. Because Mr. Wells
makes a distinction between God and his
" Veiled Being," he would distinguish this
sense of the beauty of the universe from the
sense of God. " God comes to us," he says,
" neither out of the stars nor out of the pride

of life, but as a still small voice within." But to those who have been most aware of God, He has come out of the stars and out of the lilies of the field, which are of the same order as the stars, being, like them, what we call nature. Nature, according to Mr. Wells, is an expression of the "Veiled Being," not of God; and so his God does not speak in the beauty of the earth and sky. He does not speak in beauty at all, which is merely a by-product of man's own mind. It is never the expression of a virtue that is not man's; for all nature is of the "Veiled Being," who, so far as we know, has no virtue, is in no respect of like nature with man.

On this point I can only repeat that Mr. Wells ignores the most intense religious experience of mankind, which is aware of God in nature as well as in the moral sense of mankind; and which, further, is aware of a kinship between beauty, truth, and righteousness, since it has an absolute value for all three and believes that that absolute value is for God. The religious mind does naturally and instinctively platonize; but Mr. Wells refuses to do so because, denying the immortality of the soul, he sees all life in terms of the struggle for life or for life eternal; and beauty has no

connexion with that struggle. It is, in fact,
an unintelligible luxury in the life of man.
But to the Platonist beauty affirms that life is
not all provisional, that God expresses Himself
in all things, and that man is capable here and
now of the Beatific Vision; which is a vision,
not of the philanthropic acts of God, but of
God Himself, who is to be loved as we love
beauty, not for what He does merely, but for
what He is.

According to the Christian doctrine, God
and man have this in common, that they are
immortal; according to Mr. Wells, they have
everything in common except immortality.
But the immortality of God seems, with him,
to be a mere postulate necessary to distinguish
Him from man; and, just because He is otherwise so completely human, His immortality
cuts Him off utterly from man. He is man,
but of a different species, and with one great
advantage over us which makes all His virtues
unreal. Thus, when Mr. Wells comes to speak
of the nature of God, he says, " Firstly, God is
courage." But courage, as a human virtue, is
the conquering of the fear of death. In an
immortal God it is an unreal virtue, like the
indifference of the rich man to money. When
Christianity says that God is love, it hits

upon the one virtue that is not unreal in an immortal God, that can be shared by God and man. Mr. Wells is a little suspicious of the saying that God is love. Love may mean many things, he says. But in that saying it means one thing — namely, absolute value, which, for those who see all things in terms of the struggle for life, even for life eternal, does not exist. According to the Christian doctrine love is the one virtue common to God and man, because both God and man are capable of absolute values, being both immortal. But according to Mr. Wells, since God is the one immortal being in a universe otherwise entirely occupied with the struggle for life, there are really no virtues common to God and man; and all the virtues of man, such as his courage, are in God unreal.

So his God Himself remains unreal to us, and an arbitrary exception in a universe otherwise occupied with the struggle for life. For we are occupied with the struggle for life, even though it be for the life of a remote posterity; and we value all things and all men, even God Himself, as they conduce to this life. But in the very notion of God there is implied an absolute value, not for life, but for God; and when man affirms God, he affirms his absolute value for that which has absolute value. The concept of life is empty without its content, which is absolute value, just as for Morris the social revolution was empty without its content, work for the joy of work. So when man asserts God here and now, he asserts absolute value here and now; he asserts a freedom from the struggle for life which man can attain to in absolute value even now, here, and in the flesh. His absolute values are for him an assurance of his immortality, since they are what he has in common with God. Because men can love like God, they are the sons of God, like God in their immortality, not like Him in all things except His immortality.

There is a logic in this theology which is lacking to the theology of Mr. Wells. But the great interest of his book consists in the reality and intensity of his effort to combine his own religious experience with a consistently biological conception of the universe. The effort fails, we think, but in its reality and intensity it reveals truth. For there is a truth in the biological conception of the universe which religion cannot ignore; and, when it ignores that truth, it becomes a barren game. Our virtues do arise out of the struggle for life; we know what love is from the love of a

mother for her child ; we know what fellowship
is from men's co-operation in earning their
living. The fugitive and cloistered virtue
which escapes from the struggle for life is no
virtue at all. God, whatever else He may be,
is certainly not a connoisseur of beautiful souls ;
nor is He to be found by a search for Him
which disregards men. The morality which
Mr. Wells deduces from the worship of his
God is a fine one ; and the best part of his
book is concerned with it, especially with
modern ideas of Sin. For since his God is a
leader of men and His purposes are man's purposes, sin consists in thwarting His, and man's,
purposes, and not in doing what He arbitrarily
forbids. There is this great value in the biological conception of life, that it does see
morality always in relation to some positive
purpose and not as an expression of the fear
of the unknown. It has freed morality from
taboos and cruel mysteries ; it has convinced us
that virtue is not something arbitrary and unnatural.

But at the same time it has failed to find a
firm basis for that disinterestedness which we
know to be the essence of all virtue. Mr.
Wells tells us that we are to forget ourselves
in the conquest of death. He sees all our

virtues in relation to that conquest; he sees God leading us on to it as our Captain. But all this religion and morality of his are based upon a huge assumption, that the conquest of death is something that will inspire humanity, that the soul of man can be fed upon the provisional. The Christian inspiration is the love of man as he is, of God as He is. Christianity tells man to feed his soul on that, and through that to rise above the fear of death. Its cardinal virtue, Love, is in its origin a wild virtue, the natural love of a mother for her child, the natural fellowship of men engendered in the struggle for life. This love is both animal and spiritual; it is wisdom and passion; it is the harmony of impulse and will. Compared with it, virtue, having for its aim the conquest of death, seems to be artificial, and too consciously willed. It takes too much thought for the morrow and not enough for actual people and things. It is the result of a desperate hope forced out of a conception of the universe in its essence despondent. And there is something desperate in the very virtue of Mr. Wells's God, because He is an arbitrary exception to the general nature of things as Mr. Wells conceives it. He expresses a contradiction in Mr. Wells's mind, in the whole mind of the modern world, which cannot be permanent. This is the theology of a transition; and for that reason it has a dramatic interest. The revolution has begun, but it is not, as Mr. Wells seems to think, ended, in his own mind or in any other.

Edgar Allan Poe ◠ ◠ ◠ ◠

POE'S is the strangest of reputations. His collected works fill five volumes; and a great part of them is rubbish, some of it not even clever. It is not like the hack work of a man of genius; rather, there is something provincial about it, as if it had been produced for the literary corner of a country newspaper. There is dull, long-winded criticism, accusing Longfellow of plagiarism where he had only been guilty of remembering other poets; there are comic pieces, duller still; and there are poems as bad as any man has ever written.

Yet Poe has fame, and deserves it. But his popular fame is based on poems like *The Raven* and *The Bells*, fit to be recited at penny readings. I once remarked to an American professor of literature that Poe's reputation as a poet rested on about six poems. "You mean," he answered, "*The Raven, The Bells, Ulalume, Annabel Lee?*" And I had to say as politely as possible that I meant none of these. Poe aroused wonder by an article in which he described how he wrote *The Raven*. There is nothing wonderful about it; it is just how one would expect *The Raven* to be written; but if he had written any of his poems in that manner it would have been wonderful indeed. I doubt whether he himself saw the difference between his bad and his good, between *The Raven* and *The Sleeper*. Most of his admirers have not; and the strange thing is that a man should be famous for what he wrote badly while what he wrote well is little known. It is the same with his prose. Most people have read *The Black Cat* and *The Pit and the Pendulum*; not many *The MS. found in a Bottle*, and fewer still *The Power of Words*. Yet *The Power of Words* is worth all his famous stories, including even *The Gold Beetle*, or *The Mystery of Marie Roget*; it is one of the most wonderful pieces of prose in the English language, both for manner and for matter, and, if it were the first thing of Poe's one read, one would rush to the rest of his prose expecting to find a writer of the highest rank. But one would be disappointed with nine-tenths of it; and even the other tenth would not fulfil that promise.

Edgar Allan Poe

Yet Poe has had as much influence on great writers as anyone in the nineteenth century. He influenced the young Browning in the songs of Paracelsus; and Tennyson in the most famous lyric in Maud. He influenced Morris in the *Defence of Guinevere* volume; and in prose he did at any rate originate the modern detective story, and do it better than anyone else. No man, in fact, ever had so much influence with so little to account for it. But I am at the moment concerned most with his poetic influence and with his poetic magic. For that is the only word for it. There is something magical in a very few of his poems; something that, when you fall under its spell, seems worth whole volumes of good poetry, something that takes you beyond good and evil, beyond sorrow and joy— something that all the romantic poets aimed at yet never attained to. What certainty of music there is in Swinburne! Yet one can scarcely listen to it after those few uncertain notes of Poe; for even in his best he is always uncertain. Even in *The Sleeper* there are obvious and provincial artifices. But the better one knows the poem the less one thinks of these. I should have to quote the whole of it and then ask the reader to learn it by

heart before I could hope to make him feel
its enchantment.   Yet I must quote one passage from it, so that I may tempt those who
do not know it to read the whole :—

> Oh, lady bright! can it be right—
> This window open to the night?
> The wanton airs, from the tree top,
> Laughingly through the lattice drop—
> The bodiless airs, a wizard rout,
> Flit through thy chamber in and out,
> And wave the curtain canopy
> So fitfully—so fearfully—
> Above the closed and fringèd lid
> 'Neath which thy slumbering soul lies hid,
> That o'er the floor and down the wall,
> Like ghosts the shadows rise and fall.
> Oh, lady dear, hast thou no fear?
> Why and what art thou dreaming here?
> Sure thou art come o'er far-off seas,
> A wonder to these garden trees.
> Strange is thy pallor, strange thy dress,
> Strange, above all, thy length of tress,
> And this all-solemn silentness.

It is magical by itself; but the spell of the
poem lies in the gradual discovery that the
lady is dead; and it is not a mere romantic
charnel-house spell, but the natural though
strange expression of real grief.   Poe is a
literary dandy, and a provincial dandy at that;
but there is nothing sadder than the tears of

Edgar Allan Poe

a dandy when he still keeps something of his dandified air while he weeps. This we do know about Poe, with all his airs and graces, that he suffered real sorrows, for he was possessed by a real love; and this a few of his poems would tell us if we did not know it.

To Poe this world was strange and beautiful; but there was a close, thunderous danger in its beauty. He was a strange bird in our world, and most of all in America, always homesick for a world he did not know. He talks about this life with a great display of knowledge; but, even when it is real, it is not the knowledge of a native. Try as hard as he will to be interested in it, he is homesick for a home he has never seen; and in that homesickness is his magic. How often the romantic poet tells us of his sorrows, and how seldom we believe in them, even when we enjoy his poetry. But we do believe in the sorrows of Poe as he tells them in this poem, and we wish to comfort him like a lost child.

> Take this kiss upon thy brow!
> And in parting from you now,
> This much let me avow—
> You are not wrong who deem
> That my days have been a dream:
> Yet if hope has flown away
> In a night, or in a day,

In a vision, or in none,
Is it therefore the less gone?
All that we see or seem
Is but a dream within a dream.

I stand amid the roar
Of a surf-tormented shore,
And I hold within my hand
Grains of the golden sand—
How few! yet how they creep
Through my fingers to the deep,
While I weep—while I weep.
O God! can I not grasp
Them with a tighter clasp?
O God! can I not save
One from the pitiless wave?
Is *all* that we see or seem
But a dream within a dream?

To Poe it all *was* a dream within a dream;
and never could he believe in it, even when
it brought him delight. He cared for nothing
except his wife and his art: and his wife died;
and even his art was to him a little unreal
except when he was dreaming of that home of
his which he had not seen. The greater part
of his writings he produced to make a little
money or to help him to forget the unreality
of life in mere intellectual activity. That he
could enjoy, as we enjoy games or puzzles;
and so most of his writing was to him merely a
game which he played to get money or to keep

his mind free of those thoughts which drove him towards madness. At last he drank and took drugs with the same purpose, and so died disreputable. "He was a blackguard of undeniable mark," some one said of him, as if that were all there was to be said. I wish that the complete edition of his works had not been defaced by the malignant memoir of Griswold, who misunderstood him with all the venom of stupidity. Probably Griswold suffered much from Poe, as Poe must have suffered much from Griswold; all Poe's friends must have suffered much from him. He had, Griswold says, "little or nothing of the true point of honour." His morals were not of this world, not because he was superior to it, but because he was never at home in it; and this, too, was the cause of his seeming egotism. Life hurt him at every point, and he could not forget a self that suffered so much. But why did he suffer with such powers and with every chance in his early years? There is no explanation, except that he was not born for this planet but for the star that he tells of in *Israfel*—

> Where deep thoughts are a duty,
> Where Love's a grown-up God—
> Where the houri glances are
> Imbued with all the beauty
> Which we worship in a star.

He longed for a world where intellect and passion and conscience are one; the separation between them here made each separate one of them seem to him unreal; and to live content with that tantalizing unreality was to him a servile blasphemy. He was not a common romantic; he did not turn to the false from mere incapacity to grasp the real; rather, he had a notion of a real that ought to be, hinted at in this world of shadows; and this notion, the clearer it became, made the shadows more mocking and shadowy. · He was, as his detective stories show, a man of hard intelligence. He might have been a philosopher, if there had seemed to him anything in this world worth philosophizing about; he might have been one of the few real psychologists, if he could have taken human nature seriously. But there was a fatal separation between his intellect and his emotions, except in a very few of his poems, because he could not value life or human nature in comparison with the life and the nature of that other planet for which he was homesick. So he exercised his intellect on mere games, but with a thwarted passion which gives a surprising interest and beauty even to his detective stories. One may read them once to discover the mystery of the

116

tale ; but one reads them again to discover the mystery of Poe. What kind of man was this, who could bring such powers to so trivial a task ? Perhaps there is some of that wonder even in the popularity of *The Raven*. It is a tawdry thing, but one can see the intellect through the tawdriness, the intellect which applies itself to the problem of vulgar effects as if it had a task worthy of itself. And there is always this passion in Poe even at his worst, as if he were distracting himself with trivialities from some sorrow to which he dare not surrender his whole mind. Even in *The Raven* there is one line which hints at the genius that was there wasting itself—

And each separate dying ember wrought its ghost
  upon the floor.

But Poe had a fierce desire for success at any price, together with his besetting sense of its worthlessness. There he was like Nietzsche ; he had an itch for popular applause, while he despised it. He wished to be Napoleonic in literature, to plan great coups, to use all the devices of the man of the world in art where they are futile. On one side, in fact, he was a little Byron, and in a society which had no use for Byrons great or small ; but on the other he was a slighter, more perverse, more

defenceless Shelley. And these different elements in him were incongruous, so that he
could almost spoil a poem like the *Bridal
Ballad* with romantic nonsense :—

> But he spoke to reassure me,
>   And he kissed my pallid brow.
> While a reverie came o'er me,
> And to the churchyard bore me,
> And I sighed to him before me,
> Thinking him dead d'Elormie,
> " Oh ! I am happy now."

But even this, read with the rest of the
poem, is not quite nonsense, though the dead
d'Elormie disenchants us, like nearly all Poe's
high-sounding names ; and the rest of the
poem, like *The Sleeper*, grows in beauty and
pity from the first word to the last :—

> Would God I could awaken !
>   For I dream I know not how,
> And my soul is sorely shaken
> Lest an evil step be taken—
> Lest the dead who is forsaken
> May not be happy now !

Poe can construct a poem now and again as
he constructs his detective stories, letting us
more and more into the secret with each word ;
but into these few poems he puts the whole of
his powers as he never does in his stories ; and
he puts them all into that little prose piece

Edgar Allan Poe

The Power of Words, where there is implied
the philosophy of one for whom Heaven itself
is full of desire and the passion for infinity;
for whom it is passion rather than delight,
since passion alone in this world had value for
him. There the spirits are blessed because
they see what their passions have created and
that they are not waste upon the meaningless
air. And so we feel when we read it that the
life of Poe was not waste—there was a power
in his words, and he can say, like his blessed
spirit—

This wild star—it is now three centuries
since, with clasped hands, and with streaming
eyes, at the feet of my beloved—I spoke it—
with a few passionate sentences—into birth.
Its brilliant flowers *are* the dearest of all
unfulfilled dreams, and its raging volcanoes
are the passions of the most turbulent and
unhallowed of hearts.

Worldly Wisdom 〇 〇 〇 〇

THERE is a character in Mr. Bennett's *These Twain* called Auntie Hamps, whose object is always to deceive, though she has no object in deceiving. Chicane is a habit with her, but she does not know that every one takes her chicane for granted. We have all met old ladies like her, priding themselves on their worldly wisdom but unwise in all things, trying to manage every one with a little tactful touch that exasperates more than brutality. We may itch to tell them that they are not clever at all; but we know that it would be vain. It is their pleasure in life to intrigue themselves out of imaginary difficulties, to believe that by their skill they are always escaping from dangers that do not exist. They turn life into a meaningless game and get a kind of morbid fun out of it; they are always playing patience with an imaginary adversary, and it would be cruel, if it were possible, to undeceive them.

Worldly Wisdom

These old ladies, and all those who, whether young or old, male or female, make a parade of their worldly wisdom, are survivals from a time when worldly wisdom was taken seriously as being a separate art from divine wisdom— not so lofty, but more useful. Books were written to teach it, and of these the most famous in English is Lord Chesterfield's *Letters to his Son*. But Lord Chesterfield does not take his worldly wisdom so seriously as an earlier professor of it. The classic of worldly wisdom is the *Oraculo Manual y Arte de Prudencia* of Baltasar Gracian, a Spanish Jesuit who was born in 1601, and died in 1658. It has been translated into many languages; there is an English translation of it in the Golden Treasury Series by Mr. Joseph Jacobs, from which I quote, and a German by Schopenhauer, who praised it highly. His praise makes one suspect that he knew less of the world than he thought; for Gracian, though an accomplished writer, is in his mind very like Auntie Hamps. He loves chicane for its own sake, and, though he professes to know all about the world, he is thoroughly afraid of it. It is for him a place in which you must always be on your guard, and his wisdom is all defensive.

The very headlines of his paragraphs prove this: Create a feeling of dependence—Keep matters for a time in suspense—Avoid victories over superiors—Arouse no exaggerated expectations on entering—Select the lucky and avoid the unlucky—Know how to withdraw—Think with the few and speak with the many—Use but do not abuse cunning,—all these come close together, and, though Gracian sometimes takes a higher line, they are the burden of his book. As you read it you feel, first, that worldly wisdom makes life impossible, and, next, that Gracian is not writing about it from experience. Like the German with the camel, he is evolving it out of his inner consciousness; he is as far from any reality that ever existed as a penny novelette that tells us about the wickedness of the nobility: they may be wicked, but we know they are not wicked in that way. So there may be an art of worldly wisdom; but we know that it is not Gracian's art; for his is the art of Auntie Hamps, well enough expressed, but futile in practice. Like her, he sees life as an elaborate game played according to certain rules which in real life do not exist. "Cautious silence," he says, "is the holy of holies of worldly wisdom. Mix a little mystery with everything, and the very mystery arouses veneration. You imitate the divine way when you cause men to wonder and watch." So Auntie Hamps thought; but she was mistaken. She mixed a little mystery with everything, but she did not cause men, or women, to wonder and watch. Every one saw through her mysteries, and refrained from telling her so only because of good nature. Men do not watch and wonder at those who are always trying to deceive them : they are too busy with their own affairs to be interested in a game so futile ; they shrug their shoulders and pass on to do business with some one who attends to business. Successful men of the world, even if as unscrupulous as Bismarck, reduce chicane to a minimum—they know that a lie is a last resource; but for Gracian, it is the routine of life. If we followed his advice, we should be like Metternich, according to Talleyrand, who lied always and deceived never; not like Talleyrand, according to himself, who lied never and deceived always. It is the inexperienced and the frightened who believe that cautious silence is the holy of holies of worldly wisdom. The man who is sure of himself knows that other men are clever enough, at least, to suspect caution. Even William the Silent was silent only on a famous occasion : at other times he enjoyed his own eloquence like most great men.

Gracian assumes that all other men are the enemies of the man of the world; but, if that were so, he would not be a man of the world. He assumes that worldly wisdom always takes the line of most resistance.

Man's life [he says] is a warfare against the malice of men. Sagacity fights with strategic changes of intention; it never does what it threatens, it aims only at escaping notice. It aims in the air with dexterity and strikes home in an unexpected direction, always seeking to conceal its game. It lets a purpose appear in order to attract the opponent's attention, but then turns round and conquers by the unexpected. But a penetrating intelligence anticipates this by watchfulness, and lurks in ambush. It always understands the opposite of what the opponent wishes it to understand, and recognizes every feint of guile. . . . Sagacity now rises to higher flights on seeing its artifice foreseen, and tries to deceive by truth itself, changes its game in order to change its deceit, and cheats by not cheating.

It sounds very clever; given a game with those rules, that is how you would play it. That is how Jesuits do play it in Protestant novels, and perhaps they have got their reputation

from Gracian's book. But imagine a life led
on those principles. We have only a certain
amount of energy, and we should spend it all
in deceiving and being deceived; if we aimed
always at escaping notice, we should do nothing
but escape notice, and every one would notice
us escaping it. This talk of aiming in the air
with dexterity reminds one of those Chinese
warriors who think more about the carriage of
their arms than about killing; while they are
practising their arts of war they are killed.

Gracian's error begins with his premise—
"Man's life is a warfare against the malice of
man." No doubt men often are malicious.
But malice is not their main business, nor is
it any man's main business to defend himself
against it. Malice is a risk to be taken in life;
only in war is it to be assumed, and life is not
war. You can make a war of it if you choose,
but, if you do, you certainly are not worldly
wise. This is a fact so plain that only a
professor of worldly wisdom could ignore it.
Let any man consider his chief occupations,
and he will see that they do not consist of war
against other men; at least, if they do, he is
practising them ill. The artist, the man of
science, the priest, the teacher, the physician,
the workman, the shopkeeper even,—not one

of these is at war, except by distraction from his proper business. That is to do or make things, not to prevent others from doing or making them. The tradesman may compete, but his first business, and his best way of competing, is to be a good tradesman. Even the lawyer's proper function is not so much to dispute as to compose disputes justly. Given a dispute, each side to it must be presented as clearly as possible; but a barrister who practised Gracian's arts would soon be driven from the courts by the comments of the judges. War is an attempt to impose your will on some one else, or to prevent some one from imposing his will on you. We do not spend our lives in doing either of these things, and, if we did, we should soon all be starving. Life continues with some happiness and well-being because we are, for the most part, occupied with a positive business of our own, and because we do by nature prefer that to the negative business of war. All this is evident, but not to Gracian or to Auntie Hamps; and, because it is not evident to them, they profess a peculiar art of worldly wisdom which they suppose to be different in kind from other wisdom and to be practised consciously by all men of the world.

Worldly Wisdom

No doubt Gracian had his eye on a particular world—the world of the court; but his error was in supposing it to be wise or conducted on any principles of wisdom. All men, wise or unwise, are far more spontaneous than he thinks them; and the incessant chicane of people like Auntie Hamps is the result not of design but of fear; it is the bad habit of a timid mind. No doubt in the court of a despot like Philip IV of Spain, who does not know how to rule, there is an incessant war of courtiers, all afraid of each other and all trying to rule the king; but no man need be a courtier unless he chooses, and it is not worldly wisdom to be a courtier at such a court. Yet even there Velasquez was secure without intrigue, because he was occupied with his own business and did it well. Under the worst rulers there are men who make themselves indispensable by their ability. They keep their places better by minding their business than by practising all the craft of Gracian. Olivares fell at last because of his arrogance and incompetence; he made war both abroad and at home and was defeated, but both wars were of his own making.

It was from a distant observation of such people that Gracian got his worldly wisdom;

but he begins by misunderstanding them. He supposes them to be far more deliberate and conscious than they or any men ever are. The courts of incompetent despots do not breed his kind of superman, the world itself does not breed them, and we are sure, as we read him, that he has not drawn them from life. He has seen from afar little men intriguing for little objects, and has supposed them to be great because of their rank. His superman is a monster who attains to perfection by doing what is not worth doing; whereas all excellence, even of technique, comes from doing what is worth doing.

To Gracian ability is something to be hoarded. There is no need, he says, to show it to every one. "If there is too much display to-day, there will be nothing to show to-morrow. Always have some novelty wherewith to dazzle." He thinks of ability as if it were the prepared wit of the diner-out which he must not repeat too often. He does not know that even wit grows with the exercise of it, that a witty man does not display but manifests it, and that the best wit is that which happens. Much of his advice is full of the timid malice of inexperience. "Find out each man's thumbscrew. You must know where to

get at anyone "; or, "Have a store of sarcasms
and know how to use them." But it is not
worldly wisdom to get yourself disliked, as you
certainly will if you keep a store of sarcasms
and try to find out each man's thumbscrew.
You will be known for your dirty tricks and
every one will despise you for thinking them
clever. There are people who pride themselves
on discovering the weak points of others and on
their own power of sarcasm, but they are those
who have failed in life or never tried to do
anything. There are also some able men who
cannot resist the temptation of their own
malicious wit. Lord Westbury was one of
these; but in that he was not worldly wise,
for he made enemies who turned against him
when they got the chance. In the House of
Commons nothing is hated more than sarcasm
for its own sake. It may be said that most
members do not know how to retaliate, but
there is a better reason. In our modern world
we have at least learned to stick to business;
and it is assumed that a man who hinders his
own business by saying nasty things must be
naturally malignant.

Gracian, of course, assumes this natural
malignance in every one. The world to him
is a sad, dangerous place, in which men elabor-

ate wickedness for the sake of the elaboration; they are all stage villains, and one can live among them only by learning how to frustrate them. Even the good man must defeat them with their own weapons—he cannot trust in his goodness. "The discovery of deceit," he says, "was always thought the true nourishment of a thoughtful mind, the true delight of a virtuous soul." In fact, the good man's business is to be a Sherlock Holmes; but what he is to do when he has nourished his mind and delighted his virtuous soul with detecting deceit, Gracian does not tell us. Life for him consists in deceiving and detecting; he does not seem to be aware that the mass of men have to earn their living by some kind of useful work, and have not time to be always deceiving or detecting. He is insane in his attitude towards mankind because he writes for the idle; and there again he is like a penny novelette. The art of life is for him an art divorced from use—an art that can be practised only by those who have nothing useful to do. He is romantic in a sordid way; for his people are as impossibly base as the people in the *Idylls of the King* are impossibly noble. Tennyson's sentimentality and Gracian's cynicism are both results of the romantic divorce

from business; both come from thinking of
mankind as freed from the struggle for life;
and Gracian, at least, makes us understand what
a blessing that struggle is, how it preserves us
from insanity, from insipidity, from futility.
There is always some honesty, some positive
virtue, and usually some charity, in the man
who has learned to do a useful job really well.
He does know what life is like. Knowing how
difficult his own job is, he makes allowances for
other men; he assumes that they also are
trying to do their job as well as they can and
not wasting their time in trying to deceive
each other. Perhaps the greatest virtue of the
best modern literature is that it remains conscious of the fact that the mass of men have to
earn their living, that it thinks and feels in
terms of that fact, and does not judge mankind
with the implacable fastidiousness of the idle.
The reason why Auntie Hamps is Auntie
Hamps is because she has no function of her
own in life; she has to make her own game,
and it is not as good a game as that which life
imposes on those who have to earn their living.
So Gracian assumes a paradise in which man is
free from the curse of Adam and makes of it a
silly hell.

A greater man than he was fell into the

same state of psychological error, perhaps for the same reason. We suspect that Tacitus was tempted by his own style into his portrait of Tiberius. The detection of the deceits of Tiberius was the nourishment of his thoughtful mind and the delight of his virtuous soul; but we know that Tiberius, being a man of business with a very difficult job, cannot have spent his life in deceiving other people. He may have gone mad towards the end of his life; in which case Tacitus misunderstood his madness. The Tiberius of Tacitus is the original of Gracian and all romantic pictures of impossible cunning. He has made inexperienced men of letters believe that the great world is conducted on those principles; above all, he has made them believe that cunning is far more deliberate and self-conscious than it really is, and so that it is wisdom. But no man as wise as Gracian's supermen could have got his wisdom Gracian's way. Wisdom comes of wide, passionate, and positive experience; the knowledge of men comes of loving them and confiding in them: it comes of staking all upon the nobler passions. But Gracian is always warning us against the passions; they are, he says, the humours of the soul; every excess in them weakens prudence. "Let a man be so great a master of himself

that neither in the most fortunate nor in the
most adverse circumstances can anything cause
his reputation injury by disturbing his self-
possession." No doubt there are men who
always preserve their self-possession so that
they may suffer no injury to their reputation;
but such men have no reputation to be injured.
They have emptied themselves of content so
that they may make life easy; they have lost
their souls in trying to save them. Above all,
in their excessive self-consciousness they have
cut themselves off from self-knowledge. Those
reasons which they find for their actions are
not the real reasons; behind their refusal of
all spontaneity there is a hidden spontaneity
of fear, which they will never confess to themselves, and so can never master. There is
nothing real in them except fear, and this
negative reality they could turn into a positive
only by confessing it to themselves. They are
in fact pathological; and from Gracian's book,
if we cannot learn worldly wisdom, we may at
least learn how to cure ourselves when we think
we are worldly wise.

Marvell and Vaughan ✑ ✑ ✑

IT was a happy idea of Mr. Meynell's to put
some poems of Marvell and Vaughan together
in one volume and to call it *The Best of Both
Worlds.* The very title is a light thrown on the
virtues of these two poets, on their likeness and
on the difference between them. Marvell is of
this world; Vaughan of the other; but each
gives us the best of his own world because he
is not shut up in it. There is no worldliness
in Marvell, no other-worldliness in Vaughan.
Between them, they prove that there is a
quality common to both worlds because it is
common to them. It was, indeed, the virtue
of their age to be aware of this common quality.
Many then thought and felt in terms of
both worlds; and neither religion nor science
had set up a partition between them. There
has never been a time in which so many men,
not poets by profession, have attained to the
highest excellence in poetry. It is not that,
like the Elizabethans, they had the knack of

pretty songs or were governed by a fine convention of art. The best amateur poetry of
the seventeenth century escapes from convention
and dares the utmost absurdities in its freedom ;
but the most absurd of them, Benlowes himself,
can think with the beauty of passion and feel
with the precision of thought. Writing of a
private music-meeting, he says :

> Sure it was no time to pray,
> The deities themselves then being all at play.

How could the quality of some music be better
expressed ? It is holy, but with the holiness
of gods at play. It might have been written
by Mozart about his own music, had Mozart
been a poet. All the poets of that age, from
Milton downwards, see in music the link
between the two worlds. They are of a society
in which men will at any moment gather, from
fighting or controversy or love-making or
politics, into a quiet room to make music or
listen to it. The other world, for them, is not
something to which you pay formal compliments
in church, or which you try to disprove with the
envy of those who have never seen it; it is
acknowledged, because known, by all; it shapes
gardens as it shapes music and verse; and at
any moment they could escape into its peace.

They did indeed make the best of both

worlds, because they had not cut them off
from each other, because to them beauty was
a common quality of both. Heaven was not
all mists nor earth all mud. Vaughan speaks
of the other world in terms of this one; and
Marvell of this in the terms of the other.
You can see Vaughan, in the midst of his
dreams, watching the hedges with curious eye.
It is not that he expects to see angels hiding
in them; but the beauty of the earth is to him
celestial, shaped and coloured by spirit as by
sunlight; and it speaks to him as if it were
human music. For all beauty speaks, to those
who reach a certain intensity in their appre-
hension of it. It becomes to them personal;
and they express their sense of the person in it
through what we call images or myths. But
they are neither; they are the poet's sense of
two worlds become one in beauty—of matter
seen to be spirit because it is seen to be
beautiful. This happens again and again in
all the poetry of the world; but nowhere does
it happen more naturally or with more good
faith than in the poetry of Vaughan :—

> The whole creation shakes off night,
> And for thy shadow looks the light;
> Stars now vanish without number,
> Sleepy planets set and slumber,

Marvell and Vaughan

> The pursy clouds disband and scatter,
> All expect some sudden matter;
> Not one beams triumphs, but from far
> That morning star.

In the beauty of the earth, to those who are
most aware of it, there is always expectancy;
as there is in the most beautiful music of man.
This world is looking for the other and becoming a part of it in its very expectation. That
unity of beauty, in which all things are
beautiful because they play their part in it, is
a unity of expectation; and Vaughan himself,
when he expresses it, is of it. His poetry is to
us the very mornings we have known ourselves,
when heaven and earth became one in the
fusion of mist and light; and we too were one
with the flowering sunlit sprays about our path,
and the bird-songs and flutterings, and the fall
of gleaming raindrops; all one in holy expectation. He can say that to us, without saying
it, so that we live it again and recognize it for
what it was, the marriage of earth and heaven,
the best of both worlds, only at their best
when they are thus married. He, in his own
words, was "intimate with heaven as light"
and no less intimate with earth.

Marvell, too, through his intimacy with
earth, was intimate with heaven. The world-

ling is one who sees nothing of the other world because he sees nothing of this. Thinking of everything in terms of something else, he is always glancing over his shoulder to discover what others are looking at. For him the world is like a waiting-room at Clapham Junction, where he never catches any train, but waits for pleasure or success that never comes, seeing nothing because he is always waiting. But Marvell, who had both pleasure and success, who must have enjoyed life if ever a man did, waited for nothing, but found his happiness in the garden where he was. At first it seems to be a happiness of pure sense—

> What wondrous life is this I lead !
> Ripe apples drop about my head ;
> The luscious clusters of the vine
> Upon my mouth do crush their wine ;
> The nectaren, and curious peach,
> Into my hands themselves do reach ;
> Stumbling on melons as I pass,
> Insnared with flowers, I fall on grass.

But the very intensity of sense, being enjoyed by the mind no less than the body, awakens the spirit to its own delight—

> Here at the fountain's sliding foot,
> Or at some fruit tree's mossy root,
> Casting the body's vest aside,
> My soul into the boughs does glide ;

Marvell and Vaughan

> There like a bird it sits, and sings,
> Then whets and claps its silver wings;
> And, till prepared for longer flight,
> Waves in its plumes the various light.

The very theme of this poem is that passing of sense into spirit which its' art actually accomplishes. They are not two different and hostile things as they seem to the ascetic or the materialist, both frightened fools; but rather different degrees of intensity. The poem itself is all sense, only before the theme has possessed the poet; the mind, out of the very intensity of its delight in all that the senses pour into it,—

> Creates, transcending these,
> Far other worlds and other seas;
> Annihilating all that's made
> To a green thought in a green shade.

So Shelley said of the poet :—

> He will watch from dawn to gloom
> The lake-reflected sun illume
> The yellow bees in the ivy-bloom,
> Nor heed nor see what things they be;
> But from these create he can
> Forms more real than living man,
> Nurslings of immortality.

It needed a Shelley, in his time, to see such things and to say them; and to many of his

time, and ours, his words seem mere musical
nonsense. But in Marvell's age many saw
them and said them; and they were known to
be truth. Marvell was a member of Parlia-
ment, a man of affairs; yet he had the faith,
the very experience, of Shelley, and expressed
it in a more matter-of-fact, more concrete, way,
because it was not a private faith or experience
of his own but common to many. The very
fanatics of that age were politicians and soldiers
too; they banded together and, instead of
writing pamphlets or poems published privately,
tried to practise what they preached; they
seized land on St. George's Hill at Weybridge,
and there went naked and ate no flesh.
Shelleys in action were common and talked a
religious language which, because it was religious, was the language of other men and
understood by them. So their action, because
it was religious, was but the action, carried
further, of other men and understood by them.
They were saints, not cranks, even if troublesome saints.

Marvell was not a saint or troublesome; but
he talks the language, even when he trifles, of
the extreme poets. The theme of his lines to
his coy mistress was worked to death by triflers
of succeeding generations; it had been worked

to death generations before. But for him,
even while he still seemed to trifle with it, it
was an opening to all the spaces of time and
eternity. The figures of the lover and his
mistress are like the little, modish figures of
Fragonard, which move us because their wistful
frivolity is set in a vast landscape of cloudy
golden trees and infinite avenues. There are
these avenues in Marvell's poem :—

> Had we but world enough and time,
> This coyness, lady, were no crime—

he begins like any trifling versifier, but for the
phrase " world enough and time." That phrase
controls the poem ; and he passes at once into
immensities :—

> We would sit down, and think which way
> To walk, and pass our long love's day,
> Thou by the Indian Ganges' side
> Shouldst rubies find : I by the tide
> Of Humber would complain. I would
> Love you ten years before the Flood,
> And you should, if you please, refuse
> Till the conversion of the Jews.

There follows the couplet wonderful in sound
and sense—

> My vegetable love should grow
> Vaster than empires and more slow—

a couplet that makes one think of pumpkins

and eternity in one breath, preparing for the great stroke of the poem—

> But at my back I always hear
> Time's winged chariot hurrying near;
> And yonder all before us lie
> Deserts of vast eternity.

At the end we are left wondering at this art, more like the painter's than the poet's, which can conjure everything out of nothing by its very quality. In spite of the difference of theme it is the quality of Vaughan's :—

> I saw eternity the other night,
> Like a great ring of pure and endless light,
> All calm as it was bright—

the quality of minds that know both worlds and always see one in the other.

But Marvell, the poet of this world felt to the utmost, has more of the wisdom of this world than Vaughan, and is more fit for anthologies. Most of his good poems are good all through, artfully contrived, full of audacities on the verge of absurdity and delighting us with their hairbreadth escape from it. But the best of Vaughan often suddenly trembles into life in the midst of a dead poem. It is like distant music heard suddenly in a dull street, like the other world

itself which visits us as a thief in the night.
Vaughan was always trying to write poems not
his own but Herbert's; and then he would be
forced into himself. The first poem of " Silex
Scintillans" begins thus—

> A ward, and still in bonds, one day
> I stole abroad;
> It was high-spring, and, all the way,
> Primrosed and hung with shade;
> Yet was it frost within;
> And surly winds
> Blasted my infant buds, and sin
> Like clouds eclipsed my mind.

We cannot believe in Vaughan's sense of sin
as we believe in Herbert's; the state of mind,
like the language, seems not to be his own,
except in the lines—

> It was high-spring, and, all the way,
> Primrosed and hung with shade.

So all through the poem he yields to his sense
of beauty and then drags himself away from
it that he may express Herbert's sense of sin.
But Herbert, because of the conflict in his
nature, was a psychologist and made his best
poetry out of the vicissitudes of his own mind.
Vaughan's mind is troubled only because he
cannot be always in Paradise. The fact that
Paradise comes and goes for him he imputes to

his own sin; but of the sin itself he tells us
nothing. In his most famous poem, "The
Retreat," he speaks of his own "angel-
infancy"—

> Before I understood this place
> Appointed for my second race,
> Or taught my soul to fancy aught
> But a white celestial thought.

He remembers, or thinks he remembers, a
time when he was always in Paradise; it is to
him the heavenly beauty of the earth, and the
power of being always aware of it. Then he
walked the streets of that "shady city of palm
trees" as a child-citizen, and to him religion
was the belief that he would walk those streets
again, for ever and securely. We do in memory
transform our native town into a shady city of
palm trees with celestial inhabitants; and, to
those who, like Vaughan, live on beauty and
the memory of it, heaven is not a state of
goodness merely, but the eternal presence and
full enjoyment of what is, now, always the
past. So Vaughan at his best escapes from
mere piety into this heaven, which is real to
him because he remembers it. "God's saints,"
he says, "are shining lights"; and then he
turns from this conventional phrase to his own
real religion—

Marvell and Vaughan

They are indeed our pillar fires,
Seen as we go;
They are that City's shining spires
We travel to.

He forgets the saints in the spires and in a
moment becomes a poet. When Vaughan
reaches a certain intensity of feeling both
worlds become one to him, as they do to
Shelley, to Augustine, to Marvell even. For
all these the opposition of spirit and sense is
one that happens through failure. All those
oppositions with which the mind of man is
troubled are but the result of failure to live
always at a height reached sometimes; and
what troubles them is not the opposition, but
the failure to rise above it. Vaughan is more
troubled than Marvell; for Marvell believed in
the natural man and in a simple, easy way of
life. If only men would cultivate their gardens,
they might enjoy the happiness which life
offers them with both hands—

How vainly men themselves amaze
To win the palm, the oak, or bays;
And their incessant labours see
Crowned with some single herb or tree.
Whose short and narrow-verged shade
Does prudently their toils upbraid;
While all flowers and all trees do close
To weave the garlands of repose.

If only the Kaiser had cared more for flowers than for what he called success!

But this doctrine is mere platitude, persuading no one, unless it is expressed with the poet's passion. You must yourself know the happiness this life offers you with both hands, if you are to convince others of it. Consider the lilies of the field; you must know their beauty with all your senses, if you are really to prefer them to the glory of Solomon. The very words of the saying have the beauty of the lilies in them; it is because we do not see it that we desire the vulgar glory of Solomon and fight for it. The great over-weening nuisances of the world are merely dull of sense; their energy is blind and furious because they do not know how to enjoy. Napoleon was "the unamusable." That is the wisdom which Marvell does not preach but sings. No poet is less sensual than he is; for he knows that sensuality is mere dullness of sense. Pure sense for him has the disinterestedness of spirit in it and becomes spirit as it grows more intense. That is how one world turns into the other and how the best of both becomes one. If you have the sense of beauty, which is a sense, your spirit is aware of the spirit of beauty. So he says to the Nuns of Appleton House—

Marvell and Vaughan

I see the angels, in a crown,
On you the lilies showering down ;
And round about you glory breaks,
That something more than human speaks.
All beauty when at such a height
Is so already consecrate.

See beauty with enough intensity and you see
that it is holy. You need all your sense to be
aware of spirit.

But, we may be sure, Marvell would not
have denied the more troubled and straining
doctrine of Vaughan. The language of this
world which he spoke was, because of its beauty,
kin to Vaughan's language of the other world ;
there are birds and flowers in Vaughan's
Paradise as in Marvell's garden. The same
perversity makes a man blind to both; for
he is blind to the other world because he is
blind to this one. Therefore it is well to read
these poets together, and to remember that
they lived in a time of trouble like our own, a
trouble as bitter as ours, though with a different
bitterness. Then, as now, men seemed to
make the worst of both worlds, because they
could see neither. They lived, as they live, in
a nonsense world of their own making ; and
the poets shatter it more gently, but not less
surely, than the prophets. For they show us

the true world of sense, which in their art is one. That relation which is beauty is of both worlds ; whenever you see beauty as it is—

> . . . round about you glory breaks,
> That something more than human speaks.
> All beauty when at such a height
> Is so already consecrate.

These poets, whether they trifle or agonize, are a prophecy of the human mind when it shall have learned its true business, to be aware of the one world of beauty, and to act according to its awareness. The hero rushes into the nonsense world that he may force it into sense ; the poet also has his own cure for it. He is the sun shining on the obstinate traveller ; he tells us that we have only to cast away the cloak of our own blindness and we shall see reality.

Leo Tolstoy ∽ ∽ ∽ ∽ ∽

I. THE NOVELS

THERE are few writers, even among the greatest, whom their contemporaries can without misgiving rank and compare with the masters of all ages. Leo Tolstoy, alone of the writers of our day, had this undisputed greatness. Michelangelo himself had not a higher eminence while he lived nor one more certain not to be abased by time. The very fact that Tolstoy writes in a language which few understand, except those whose native tongue it is, makes us the more secure in our admiration of him. Since we can only read his works in translation and robbed of all their native graces of execution, we know that they do not beguile us with any unessential or transient beauties. It must be some greatness in the man himself that exalts the bare sense of what he writes above sense and style together in the works of lesser men. But it is only in some of his writings that this greatness is apparent to all, only as a novelist that he is an undisputed master; and now it is of his novels alone, and in particular of *War and Peace* and *Anna Karenina*, that I shall speak. His mind, in its strange and troubled journey towards a goal hidden from us and perhaps from himself, left his novels far behind; and he came to think little of literature in comparison with preaching; but here I am concerned only with literature.

Though Tolstoy's genius is so plain to all, it has no threatening sublimity like the genius of Michelangelo. His works move us like epic poetry; but they are written in quiet prose, as far removed from poetry as any good prose can be. They do not overawe us with their greatness, but gently persuade us of it; they do not make us impatient of reality, but reconcile us to it. Nothing seems to be heightened or arranged in their world, which, though it is Russian, grows more familiar to us than the world of Anthony Trollope. They are full of details, which if related by anyone else would seem tedious or absurd, but which, as Tolstoy tells them, have an inexplicable significance, working upon our minds like the great passions and events of tragic poetry and by a process which, if it is slower, is more sure.

Leo Tolstoy

We take it for granted that prose is inferior to poetry and the novel to the epic or the tragedy; and, indeed, nearly all novels, even of the greatest writers, are inferior; for they have not altogether found a law of their own, but are still to some extent subject to the alien law of the theatre or of narrative poetry. Either they aim at dramatic climaxes and a dramatic symmetry of plot, or else they are controlled by a poetic principle of selection. But Tolstoy has justified the novel as a form of art, and placed it upon a level with epic and tragedy by freeing his plots from all dramatic climaxes and symmetry, and by working upon his own prose principle of selection. The novel in his hands does not try to do what can be better done in a play or a poem. It does something different; and it reveals advantages to compensate for its inherent defects. It is impossible that a novel should express or communicate so intense an emotion as an epic or a tragedy; but the emotion of Tolstoy's novels, if less intense, seems to be more reasonable and more closely connected with life as we know it; there is not less of it, but it is more diffused. In all poetry most of the routine of life must be left out; we see epic and tragic characters, even Hamlet himself, only at carefully chosen

moments of exceptional experience. But we
see Levin, in *Anna Karenina*, engaged in the
very routine of life, doing things that could
not be described in poetry. We see him
packing up before his wedding, and mowing,
not like an epic hero to the admiration of his
hinds, but rather indifferently. Now, it is
quite true that routine is described in other
novels, but very seldom so as to move the
reader to a serious emotion. Either it is made
fun of, or else it is only introduced because it
is necessary to the machinery of the plot. No
other novelist has Tolstoy's power of investing
it with a profound significance, because none is
so constantly moved to emotion himself by all
the details of life. And this emotion in
Tolstoy is never sentimental. He does not
force it for the purposes of his art; he does
not pretend to see more in life than he does
see, nor affect any preternatural sensibility or
sagacity. He writes as if his readers were his
equals, and as if his business was to supply
them with facts, not with emotions or per-
ceptions. Just as we all find it difficult to be
just and wise and calm and entirely serious in
dealing with the ordinary routine of our lives,
so novelists have the same difficulty in dealing
with routine in fiction. But Tolstoy is happy

Leo Tolstoy

with it; he seems to have experienced it with
the sensibility of a poet, with the calmness of
a philosopher, and with the attention of a man
of business. His knowledge of all kinds of
affairs is immense, and he never displays it as
if he had acquired it for the purposes of his
art. He writes of war like a soldier, of politics
like a politician, of farming like a farmer, yet
never with the narrowness of a specialist, but
always as if he saw the relation of these things
to the whole of life, and as if that relation
were what mainly interested him in them.
And it is the same with his characters; in
most good novels there are one or two characters that seem to come out of the writer's
own personal experience, to be autobiographical,
while the rest are the result of external
observation. But nearly all Tolstoy's characters, male and female, important and un-
important, seem to be autobiographical, and
not conjectured, but known. He does not
write, even of his most delightful girls, even of
Nataasha or Kitty, as if he were in love with
them, but rather as if he had once been a
delightful girl himself. There is never any of
the excitement or romance or mystery of sex
in his treatment of women; but only the
romance and mystery of life. And thus he is

as much interested in the old mother as in the young girl, and gives her equal rights in his story. Sometimes even he fails with his characters. Fashion is the one thing he cannot understand or endure. Thus he makes nothing of Helen, the wife of his hero, Peter, in *War and Peace*; he dislikes her so much that he does not even wish to understand her. And Vronsky in *Anna Karenina* is only a kind of Steerforth executed with more care but less spirit; one cannot believe that Anna could have fallen in love with him. Then he has an obvious prejudice against doctors and philosophers and Napoleon Bonaparte; and, when he yields to this, the great world of his creation fades away from him and leaves him preaching. But he never attempts to conceal his prejudices; and they only make him unjust in his own person, not in his conduct of events. Though they may interrupt his narrative for a little while, they do not pervert it; he soon gives over preaching and becomes the unrivalled novelist again.

Complaints have been made that there is no clear and consecutive story in his novels, and particularly in *War and Peace*. And, indeed, no reader can be drawn through them by a desire to learn what is going to happen next;

for in them we are interested in what is
happening, it never occurs to us to speculate
about the future, since we are absorbed in the
present. We do not ask ourselves what Tolstoy
is going to do with Peter or Levin; we watch
to see what they are doing with themselves.
The significance of these books is not in the
story but in the characters, who seem to control
whatever story there is. Thus, when a character appears, our interest in him does not
depend upon his relation to the story, and is
not suspended until that relation is established;
the moment he is introduced we watch him
for his own sake. Whatever he says or does
holds our attention, not for the light it throws
upon the plot, but for the light it throws upon
him. The characters, whether they persist all
through the book or only appear once or twice,
have an independent life of their own, like real
men and women. In nearly all novels we know
that when something happens it will be used
to further the story; and thus we are on the
look-out for hints as to how the story is going.
We can foretell the course of events far better
than in real life, for we know the ways of
novelists better than those of Providence.
But in Tolstoy's novels this prophetic power
fails us. We cannot tell how events will affect

the plot or whether they will affect it at all. They are not linked together in an artificial chain of cause and effect; and if we trust to them to hold our attention we shall be disappointed.

Yet it is a great pleasure to feel in these novels that we are free from this artificial chain of iron necessity, though we may be bewildered for a while before we get used to our freedom. In particular, it is delightful to find that the consequences of a wrong or foolish act do not attend the unfortunate doer of it all through the story. In other novels, even if the circumstances of retribution are exciting, they often irritate us, because we feel that the retribution is more exact than in real life. And, after all, who is the novelist that he should pretend to know the just punishment for all offences, especially when he uses that punishment to make his plot? Real life is often troublesome enough; but it would be more troublesome if it always punished and awarded according to human ideas of justice. Whatever Tolstoy's ideas of justice may be, he does not let them control the story; he is content to leave vengeance to God, and will not tamper with probabilities to hasten it. That agreeable sinner, Stepan, who in most novels would

come to a bad end, in *Anna Karenina* comes to
no end at all. He is only perpetually interesting, and, for all his sins, perpetually delightful.
He is one of those people whose society in real
life we all enjoy; and so we enjoy it in *Anna
Karenina*. Such men are usually rewarded in
real life for the pleasure which they give. The
world likes them and will not conspire to
punish them; so Stepan is not punished by
the world. Tolstoy will not tell lies even to
point a moral; and he himself likes Stepan as
Macaulay likes Charles II.

These stories may seem inconclusive to
readers who demand that destinies shall be all
settled at the end of a story. But they are
only satisfied at the end of the ordinary novel by
a mere convention. They would know, if they
cared to think, that happiness is not assured
to the hero and heroine by marriage, however
much they may be in love. The novelist says,
or implies, that they lived happy ever after;
but that is only that he may find an excuse to
have done with them. In tragedy there is a
real end; and destinies are settled, at least for
this world, by death. But Tolstoy feels that
there is a great deal in life of vast significance
besides tragedy and besides what is conducive
or subordinate to tragedy. You cannot say

that *War and Peace* is a sad book or a merry one, any more than you can say that life in general is merry or sad. You feel as you read it that life is not to be judged by its pleasures or pains, nor by any ordinary standard of failure or success. It has some unseen goal, and men are moved by some unknown force towards it, and by inexplicable passions when they think of it. Every detail of the book, however trivial it may seem, is chosen to illustrate the working of that force and of those passions. For Tolstoy, though he cannot tell us what the goal is or the force that draws us towards it, is himself constantly and intensely aware of both. It is the peculiarity of his genius that he combines this mystical consciousness of what life desires to be with a vast curiosity and knowledge of what it is. Mystics are apt to be impatient of the routine of life, of everything in which the purpose of life, as they conceive it, is not clear and strong. But Tolstoy has sought for that purpose with a scientific ardour and patience, not only in the ecstasies of his own mind or in the noblest works of God and actions of men, but also in all that men do when they seem to be the slaves of circumstance and of their own habits and errors and appetites. The scientific conscience is so predominant now that sometimes it seems to threaten art and even morals. In Tolstoy's novels, it is the friend and willing servant of both; indeed, his art, his morals, and his science seem to be all one, or only different aspects of the same power in him. His incessant and impartial observation of fact has not weakened his sense of purpose, but confirmed it; and his realism has not made his books squalid or incoherent, but only given them a beauty more reasonable and secure, a unity more natural and unforced. As we read them we feel that they tell the whole truth about life, with nothing extenuated and nothing set down in malice; and at the end we are more in love with life than ever before. The great tragic poets show us the glory of life triumphing even in death. Tolstoy does what is even harder and more comforting. He shows us the glory of life triumphing in the midst of its own failures and squalor and wearisome routine.

Leo Tolstoy ✿ ✿ ✿ ✿ ✿

II. Tolstoy and Russia

IN Mr. Aylmer Maude's book on Tolstoy he
says many things that he would not have
said or thought but for the Russian disaster.
Tolstoy is the Rousseau of the Russian Revolution. It would have happened, no doubt, in
some form or other, if he had never been born,
but not in the form it has taken. His ideas,
however much misapplied, inspire it. Lenin
and Trotsky were supported in their fresh
desire for peace at any price, by multitudes
who had learned from Tolstoy to hate war;
and all the intellectuals of Russia learned from
him to believe that the institutions, not only of
Russia, but of all Europe, are wicked and
absurd. To them society is not a living thing,
that must continue to live even while an
operation is performed on it; the operation is
more important than society. Men are in a
wrong relation altogether; free them from

that relation and all will be well. But it does not seem to most of us that all is well in Russia. So we are all of us, Mr. Maude included, more ready to criticize the teaching of Tolstoy than we were when he died. Most of us felt that there was something wrong with that teaching, even if we could not find the flaw in his logic; we were not disposed to accept it; and we are, unconsciously, glad to discover that it fails when put in practice.

Of course, Tolstoy himself would have a ready answer to our criticism based on results. He was against all force, and the Bolshevists use force; they are false to the most essential point of his teaching. But to that answer another may be made. The resolve to use no force does in fact lead to anarchy, in which nothing but force prevails. It is vain to say that men ought to be able to live without force; they are of such a nature that they cannot; and the proper aim of society is not to abolish force, but to reduce it to a minimum. Mr. Maude sees that clearly; he sees that there is something mischievous in Tolstoy's teaching, something poisonous to the minds of men less strong, less passionate, less able, than he was. It is not merely a matter of difficulty of application; the doctrine itself must be wrong if the attempt to practise it leads to disaster, for doctrines exist so that they may be practised, they exist in relation to the facts of man's nature; and, where they ignore those facts, they are false.

What, then, is the error of Tolstoy's doctrine? Mr. Maude says that "the duty of man is not to do what he can't, but to do the best he can." There is a moral obligation on all moral teachers to discover the best that man can do, not to set impossibilities before him, and to tell him that, if he does not perform them, he is damned. For impossibilities, because they are impossibilities, are wrong. Our problem is not to discover what we ought to do if we were different, but what we ought to do, being what we are. There is no end to the beings we can imagine different 'from ourselves; but they do not exist, and therefore we cannot assume that they would be better even than we are if they did exist. With them we have to assume a whole reality that is not; and that reality, since it is a figment of our minds, would probably be inferior to the reality that is. For there is this to be said in favour of reality, that we have nothing to compare it with. Our phantasies are always incomplete because they are phantasies, and reality is complete; we cannot compare their incompleteness with its completeness. So the beings we imagine different from ourselves are incomplete. The Bolshevists perhaps have tried to be the beings that Tolstoy imagined; but they remain in reality as it is, and they cannot, in that reality, perform the impossibilities that he demanded of them.

There was in Tolstoy a dislike of reality, which included a dislike of men as they are and of himself as he was. Like many other reformed rakes, he became a Manichee, believing that the flesh in man is the enemy of the spirit and that there can be no truce between them. *The Kreutzer Sonata* is the most obvious expression of his Manicheeism; in it he sees sexual desire as bad in itself, as always a temptation of the flesh to the spirit; and for him it makes no difference whether those who desire each other are married or unmarried. Mr. Maude quotes a remark of the hero Pozdnishev which illustrates this. A lady says to him: "But you are speaking of physical love. Don't you admit the existence of love founded on identity of ideals and spiritual affinity?" And Pozdnishev replies: "Spiritual affinity! Identity of ideals! But in that case (excuse my rudeness), why do they go to bed together ? " Pozdnishev and Tolstoy, and all Manichees, hold that there is a necessary incompatibility between sexual and spiritual love, and that the one destroys the other; and *The Kreutzer Sonata* was written to maintain that. According to Tolstoy, the flesh is sinful, foul, ugly in itself; a man must kill it if he is to attain to any freedom of the spirit. He never grasped the idea that flesh is the necessary medium of spirit, that through desire men and women come to love. But if that is true of flesh and spirit in sexual matters, it is true of flesh and spirit in all things. The struggle for life exists, in all its forms; it is the medium, the necessary condition, of spirit. But to Tolstoy it was merely evil, and he told men to give it up altogether; which is impossible. All those institutions which are based on a recognition of the struggle for life as a fact— property, law, government—were to him evils; just as the means by which the human race is propagated were to him evils. He did not wish to make them more completely mediums for spiritual life, he wished to abolish them altogether; nor did he care in the least what would happen if they were abolished. Mr. Maude quotes a saying of his to a friend : " If your starting-point and deductions are sound, never be afraid of practical objections to your logical conclusions. Otherwise you will never say or produce anything original." Yes! but practical objections warn us that our starting-point or our deductions are not sound. If a man of science makes an experiment which fails, he concludes that there is something wrong with his science, not with the nature of the universe. Tolstoy concluded always that there was something wrong with the nature of man, not with his science. He warred against the nature of man; he told men to do what was contrary to their nature; and, when they failed to do it, he washed his hands of them. Not in practice; no one can accuse him of indifference or of not trying to practise what he preached; but his theory remained right, and men remained wicked.

For this Manichee state of mind the wickedness is always in those who govern, who maintain society as it is; but for them men might escape from their chains. So that the Manichee may not utterly despair of human nature, he makes a figment of the natural man, who is prevented from being natural by those who govern him. Government, to Tolstoy, is something imposed on mankind; institutions are all imposed on mankind arbitrarily from outside, by a few perverse persons in whom is concentrated all sin. If only the natural man could free himself from these he would live well. Tolstoy never saw that government and all institutions are not impositions but growths, except where one nation conquers and tyrannizes over another. There may be, and always is, evil in them ; but it is not the evil only of the few governors, it is not the result of a conspiracy ; it is the evil of a whole society expressing itself in its institutions or in the working of them. The Russian Government was corrupt because corruption is a vice of Russians, not because it was government. In Russia the natural man is corrupt, not merely the unnatural rulers ; and so it is with the vices of government everywhere. Where they persist, it is because the people consent to them, not because government in itself is evil. The evil remains when government is removed.

The Manichee in Tolstoy wished to remove from human nature an essential fact in that nature, an essential fact in all life, as we know it. He wished to remove the flesh which is the very medium of the spirit, despairing of a harmony between them. He did not see that men learn fellowship from co-operation in the struggle for life, and love of wife and children through desire. For him, though he would not confess it, there was a malice in the very nature of things which made spirit and flesh enemies for ever. God, to him, was He who commands man to do what he cannot do, not He who has made matter a medium for the spirit of man. So the problem of life was not, to him, a problem of gradual expression but one of sudden renunciation. More and more he took a disgust of the very facts of life, suppressing his own strong natural relish for those facts; and he condemned all his own greatest works because they expressed that relish. In his *What is Art?* he condemned the artist, said that he had no right of his own to exist; he was to be judged by his effect on the natural man, that figment of Tolstoy's own mind, and always by his moral effect. As Mr. Maude says :—

For Tolstoy the great importance of art to mankind lies in the fact that through its manifold forms . . . we are infected (for good or evil) by feelings that the artists have experienced and transmitted to us. In this way we may become united in feeling, and in our minds the rails are laid along which our actions will naturally pass.

"For good or evil" here means for moral good or moral evil; art is to be judged finally by the actions which it produces. Therefore, if it is not understood by the mass of men and so produces no action in them, it is bad art; its whole function is to produce good, moral action. Now this we know to be absurd, even if we cannot state the absurdity. We do not judge art by the actions it produces, for we do not know what actions it will produce when we judge it. We judge it not in terms of morals at all, but by its immediate effect on ourselves; and we do not ask whether or not some one else will be able to understand it. According to Tolstoy, we ought to take a Russian peasant with us to a performance of the Choral Symphony, and, if it is nonsense to him, that must make it nonsense to us. But the effect of art on us is beauty; and, when we find beauty in it, we do not ask whether others find beauty in it, or what the moral effect of that beauty will be. We trust in the God of beauty, who was not God at all to Tolstoy, because he became a Manichee and feared beauty as being of the flesh. But beauty is of the spirit and the flesh, it is that harmony of both which Tolstoy despaired of. Naturally therefore he was impatient of the very word and said that it meant nothing, since he could not find its meaning in moral terms, since he could find no help in it for his struggle to overcome the flesh. The very lesson of beauty, if we need one from it, is that spirit and flesh are not enemies, but that one is the medium of the other. When matter is the medium of spirit, there is beauty; and we do not need to ask what is the moral use of that harmony; it is good in itself, good to us, even though a Russian peasant may not be able to see it.

The fact is that Tolstoy did a violence to himself, forced himself from his proper business in life, and suffered in his whole nature from that violence. He is not to be condemned for this perversion of himself, which was indeed heroic; but we need to be aware of it, if we are to understand his ideas and the error that is in them. Tolstoy had artistic, but not religious, genius. There is in his art a wonderful ease and richness, but in his religion, and his writings upon it, an arid and painful logic. That passion, which was free in his art, in his religion turned against itself, feared itself and the whole nature of the universe. In his very refusal to consider the practical effect of his doctrines there was fear, as there is in all fanaticism, a fear not of men—he was far above that—but of himself and of God. He could not trust himself without the help of rigid dogma; and he conceived of this dogma as imposed on him by God. It is strange that, with all his scorn of the dogmas of the Church, he should not have seen that he wished to subdue the soul of man to a worse slavery. He saw himself as a creature of stubborn and evil will that must be subdued by obedience to command. The problem of life for him was the subduing of his own passions; and he saw all life in the light of this problem. We do not know how much of a rake he was in his youth—men of his nature often make themselves out to have been worse than they were—but we do know that he was fierce, obstinate, irritable, contemptuous, and always repenting of those faults. His genius could not content him; he was angry with those writers, especially Turgenev, who glorified the artist. When he asked, "What do I know? What do I teach?" they said that the artist teaches unconsciously. "I was considered an admirable artist; and therefore it was very natural for me to adopt this theory." But soon he began to doubt the infallibility of this religion. He was forty-six when his doubts became an inexorable trouble to him. Then he said to himself, "Very well; you will be more famous than Gogol or Pushkin or

Leo Tolstoy

Shakespeare or Molière, or than all the writers
in the world; and what does it lead to? And
I could find no reply at all. Had a fairy come
and offered to fulfil all my desires, I should not
have known what to ask." Life seemed to him
meaningless, and he had to find a meaning in it.
It was emptied of values, and he had to fill it
again. "I could find nothing along the path
of reasonable knowledge except a denial of
life; and in faith I could find nothing but a
denial of reason, still more impossible to me
than a denial of life."

At last, like so many men thus afflicted, he
saw that he must deny neither life nor reason,
but himself. But denial of self is a phrase;
and there was error in his self-denial which it is
hard to detect and state exactly. It was more
negative than positive. That hard, fierce
troublesome self of his was to him altogether
an enemy; and be wished to destroy it rather
than to transmute it. Self-denial became for
him an end in itself rather than a means to an
end; and he wished it to be an end for all men.
The aim of religion is self-forgetfulness in the
glory of the universe; to that Tolstoy never
attained securely, to the last he saw life in
negative terms. He subdued himself to
dogma that said—Thou shalt not; and never

reached the positive joy beyond. There is the reason of his condemnation of art; for art expresses that positive joy and says that it is good in itself. But to Tolstoy what art expresses was not good in itself; it was but a means to an end; and even his art must be the slave of his dogma, like himself. So he attracted fanatics to him; and was puzzled to find that he did not like them; for he remained always greater than his own dogmas, and tender to those who could not obey them, since he never could obey them utterly himself.

Mr. Maude makes us see that to the end he was, in himself, the Tolstoy of the great novels, a man and not a walking theory. His conflicts were always real; and he would be content with no easy victory of logic. He set himself and mankind an impossible task; he made a diagram of life and tried to live according to it; but his sympathies were still with men like himself, too rich of nature to live according to any diagram. He tried to deny his own sense of beauty, his own humour, his own passion, but he could not destroy his own kindliness. And it was the conflict between dogma and love that made the tragedy of his last days. Of that Mr. Maude gives a very clear account; according to him, Tchertkof was Tolstoy's evil genius, the arid fanatic that he tried, and failed, to be himself. It was Tchertkof who put his dogmas into practice and reduced them to an absurdity. At the end, when he had fled from his home to die, and feared lest his wife should follow him, he said to Tchertkof— "You understand that, if she comes here, I shall not be able to refuse her," and he began to cry. There is a last instance of the struggle that raged within him and never came to an end, the struggle between dogma and human feeling. Then he said, "Evidently I shall have to die in my sins." And Tchertkof replied, "This is not sin, but love, that now surrounds you. You have done all you could to escape from sin." That was the best Tchertkof could say; he, too, saw all life as an escape from sin, and it meant to him Tolstoy's escape from his wife. But Tolstoy himself, you may be sure, was not satisfied. His last words in his diary were: "I see our plans have failed. . . ." His last words were—"To escape . . . To escape." His wife was not allowed to see him until he was unconscious.

It cannot be pretended that he died happy. He had given himself over to the power of fanatics lesser than himself, who denied him what his heart most desired. So it is now with his country; and its cry, too, must be—"To escape; to escape." The greatest of Russians was in his whole life a prophecy of his country. The richest of gifts, never freedom; a conversion, a revolution, and after it not the freedom it seemed to promise but slavery to dogma worse than the slavery to passion. And in the case of Russia, as of Tolstoy, we are sad, but we do not judge; with neither can we see the end. Both know more conflict, more suffering, than other men or nations; both seem to disappoint those who expect most of them.

We cannot prophesy the future of Russia any more than we can prophesy the future of Tolstoy; but we can refrain from judging. Mr. Maude, in his book, gives us the facts, but does not judge; he makes us feel that here is a greater than ourselves, greater not only in art but in character; in the very enormity of his errors there is greatness. His life was not finished here; it was broken off with that unsatisfied cry—"To escape; to escape." So for us the life of Russia is not finished; her failure is not final; in the future she may win freedom and peace for herself and enrich the world with the fruit of all her sorrows.